Retail Rebellion

How To Create Your Own Online Retail Empire

2013 Edition

By Nathan & Tessa Hartnett

Retail Rebellion – How To Create Your Own Online Retail Empire

© 2013 Nathan & Teressa Hartnett

Acknowledgments

We'd like to thank all of our supporters over the years, through the good times and the bad. Particularly our families who supported everything we've done, and the decisions we've made. We would especially like to thank HMB!

Before You Read This Book!

Hi and welcome to the introduction for Retail Rebellion. Before we get started, we need to explain what this book is, and also what it isn't. Retail Rebellion is our business model in a book. It will give you all of the ingredients you need to significantly increase your chances of succeeding with niche e-commerce. It is however, a recipe.

Tess came up with the analogy of baking a cake. You can't just choose to use some ingredients and not the rest, and still expect to come out with the same cake that we have. Secondly, what this book is not. It's not a manual that will guide you through all aspects of e-commerce online.

For example, if you want an in depth look at all of the different payment types or e-commerce platforms out there, this is not the book to show you. We don't claim to be experts in every aspect of e-commerce, but we do claim to be successful using the business model contained in this book, and we hope that it helps you succeed where so many have failed.

If you currently own an e-commerce business, we believe that you can learn a lot from this book, however you must understand that choices you've already made in your business may affect the success you'll have when applying some of the principles found here. As an existing e-commerce owner, you may find it more difficult to use our model, simply because a large part of our success comes with our product and niche choice right from the beginning.

This book is also best used in conjunction with our series of workshops that show you exactly how to do the "grunt work" involved with setting up your site. From registering domain names to building the site itself, you can save yourself a lot of time and money by simply following our videos and guides. You can find them at www.talknbusiness.com.

After reading, you can also contact us at www.talknbusiness.com with any questions that you feel the book doesn't answer, and we'll be happy to help.

Who are we?

Our names are Nathan and Tessa Hartnett, and we started looking for our first online retail business idea back in 2005. At the time, Nathan was an Air Traffic Controller, and Tess was studying to be a school teacher – two careers very far from the online retail world! We had great incomes, the respect of our peers, and were doing everything we were told we were supposed to, but still weren't satisfied with our lives. We were facing that all important question of, "is this it?"

We knew there was a whole world out there that we wanted not just to see for a couple of weeks every year, but to truly experience. We wanted to spend our days together, we wanted to live overseas, and most importantly, we wanted to be able to get out of bed every morning and choose what we did that day.

Because of our particular desire to travel and live overseas, we needed to find a source of income that would allow us to be "location independent", and because of our desire for time and choice, it also needed to be passive.

While there were plenty of "Get Rich Quick Online" offers out there, many of which didn't require a physical product, we wanted to be able to prove a market existed before we started spending money, and at the time, the only way we could find to do this was through eBay's completed listings (which we'll discuss in further detail in a later chapter). This is the main reason we started with a physical product, and why we went on to create a business that would ultimately evolve into VurgeJewellery.com.

Since we started the business, we have lived in Christchurch, New Zealand (the South Island of New Zealand is possibly the most beautiful place on earth) for nearly two years, and are now living in Bangkok, Thailand (possibly the most crazy and fun City on earth!). Our businesses support us both full time, and we have recently launched another eight new online retail businesses.

Tess recently became Alibaba.com's Female Ambassador, and has spoken at the two biggest online retail conferences in Australia.

We have been blessed with the lifestyle of our dreams, and are hoping to share what has taken us years of experimenting, failing, and succeeding to learn. This is the book we wish we had available so many years ago. We hope you enjoy!

Table of Contents

Chapter 1 - Why Online Retail?

Since entering the world of business in 2005, we've tried a number of different models including affiliate sites, information products, offline retail, weekend markets, even party planning! In the end though, we still have found ourselves back to where we started with online retail. Why? Because that's what makes us money, and gives us the lifestyle we set out to achieve. There is no doubt that other business models can work for some people, and more power to them for doing it, but online retail using the methods we share in this book is relatively low cost, low risk, and highly scalable. Like any business model though, it can also be a money pit if done incorrectly.

The idea of starting a new business in 2012 is a scary one for many people – and it should be. The Global Economy is trapped in a financial malaise that is difficult to see through, and the future is anything but certain. This is exactly why you should be looking for alternative sources of income, but why you should be very cautious about every dollar that you spend trying to achieve them.

Any entrepreneurial endeavor involves risk, but it should be managed. A famous British Entrepreneur (who is known for his risk taking) once said that while you can never completely eliminate risk, you should do everything you can to reduce it, and to manage it.

So risk is inevitable, but you can reduce it through educating yourself, and what we call "scaling in" to the business using the concept of minimum viable product, which will be discussed in much greater detail in later chapters.

So online retail is low cost of entry, it is easier to prove a market than just about any other business, and it is relatively low risk (especially when compared to offline retail!). What is the opportunity? Isn't retail crashing with the current economy? Offline retail certainly is, with malls becoming vacant, and many retailers going out of business in most of the western world. This is why it is so important to understand the structural differences between online and offline retail (something that seems so basic on the surface – but we still had to learn the hard way). Part of the reason offline retail is doing so poorly, is *because* of online retail. Online retail in the U.K. grew at 14% in 2011, while in the U.S. it grew 16.1%, and in Australia it grew at a staggering 23%!

There is a pretty obvious reason why this is occurring. Online retailers have much lower costs than offline retailers (if done correctly), and can therefore offer a much greater value proposition. Consumers who previously were a bit wary of buying online are now being driven online by the promise of greater savings (as their spending power diminishes), as well as a growing comfort level with using the internet in general. In other words, the worse things get economically, the better it will be to have your own online business(es) going. And if things improve economically, it doesn't matter because "the cat's out of the bag" and once people have tasted the convenience and value proposition of online shopping, they won't rush back to the shopping mall anytime soon.

The one obvious drawback of online retail (as opposed to online information products) is that you still have stock to deal with, and logistical issues. There are ways to overcome these hurdles though, as we have, and we believe that if you follow the advice in this book, you will be able to as well.

Another reason why we prefer online retail to other forms of online business is that Google tends to like us a bit more. With our information based businesses, you are constantly fighting the "Google Monster", and every time Google does an update, you can watch your business change overnight – usually not for the best.

With our retail businesses however, all we ever seem to see are improvements in our rankings, even though they are gradual. As far as search engine rankings are concerned, it's a far less stressful model. This is because Google wants to be putting professional, well branded, relevant websites at the top of their rankings and keep them there. Once upon a time, it was pretty common to do a search for "blue widgets" in Google, and many of the results would be small information sites about blue widgets that then had paid links to other sites that actually sold blue widgets. Google has declared war on these types of sites, as it's reasonably sure that when someone searches for "blue widgets", they want to go straight to a site that actually sells blue widgets.

So do you want to be the business that Google wants to give traffic to in future? Or do you want to be the site that Google is trying to stamp out?

Who Is This Book For?

This book was written to provide a holistic approach to starting niche online retail businesses. If you are brand new to the world of making money online, then we hope to provide you with a business model that will not only help you to be successful, but to also minimise the startup costs and associated risks.

If you are quite familiar with online business models, but haven't quite been as successful as you'd like, we're providing you with the model that has proven itself to us, and we have no doubt that we can save you time, money and a lot of headaches.

If you are an offline retailer looking for a guide on how to get your product online, we have no doubt that you will find a great number of helpful tips in this book, but please be careful. Much of the success you have in online retail comes down to the product you select, whether or not online purchasers want to buy it, and how much competition there is online. For anyone who currently has a product, or even has a product in mind that they'd like to sell online – do not skip the product selection chapters. If your current product fails any of the tests that we put our product ideas through, then it's time you considered changing what product you sell. This may be hard to accept for a business owner who has a warehouse or store full of unsold stock that they want to sell online, but there is zero point in "flogging a dead horse". It will just cost you more money, and create more stress in your life.

Whatever your background is, you're no doubt reading this book because you want to make a change in your life. This was our primary motivation in starting, and we've been fortunate enough to be able to do just that. Above all else we wish the same for you, so let's get started!

Chapter 2 - Where Do I Start?

Finding The Right Product

This is the part where people can either get stuck in "analysis paralysis", or end up at the other end of the spectrum where they get too impatient, and choose a product based on false analysis. This almost always leads them to losing time and money. First let's deal with how to find a product.

This chapter should really be entitled "How To Find A Market", because that is what you are really looking for. So many businesses fail because the founder has either invented a product, or has a unique twist on a product that he/she thinks the rest of the world will love, and that it will make them a millionaire. It's often said in the business world that if you want to be successful in business, don't invent something. If you do invent something, you'll have to spend big money to make the world actually care, and if (this is the biggest if of them all) somehow you do make them care, then your competitors will come into the market overnight, and take over much of your market share. In other words, you'll be doing all the work, while others will end up taking much of the gain.

Did Apple invent mp3 players? No. Did Microsoft invent PC Operating Systems? No they didn't. The list is endless. The risk of trying to bring a new product to market is massive, so we wouldn't recommend it at all, unless you are extremely well funded, and are happy to gamble this money on a faint possibility of wild success.

So this is why we want to find an established market. One where enough people know about the type of product, value its benefits, and are searching for someone to supply it to them in a manner and format that is suitable for them. As far as the online space is concerned, it's the word "searching" that is most relevant. Back in the old days, it was very difficult (and costly) to find out what products people were interested in, and what they valued. The only way to do it was through surveys and focus groups, and even these were fraught with poor data issues.

I remember reading about one focus group study that was done to determine whether or not people would buy a particular product at a particular price, and overwhelmingly the group said that yes, they loved the product, the price was right, and they would buy one if it was on the market. The organiser of the focus group then told the group that it was their lucky day, because they just happened to have the product available right then and there, with full EFTPOS and Credit Card facilities. None of the group bought the product. This is just one example of how a focus group or survey can present wildly inaccurate results, because because participants will often say "yes" to please those around them, but when it comes to actually parting with their hard-earned cash, the answer is "no thanks".

Fortunately, we live in an age where you can not only determine the size of the market for particular products far more accurately, but you can do it in a couple of minutes, and it's absolutely free.

We do it by using a program called "Long Tail Platinum", but you can also do it using Google's Keyword Tool. This tool was designed by Google to show potential advertisers the audience reach that they would be getting by advertising with Google, but you can use it too. You can find it by searching for "Google keyword tool", and it will be the number one result. While you can use it without an adwords account, we definitely recommend signing up. It's free, and means that you will get 800 results instead of 100, and it also means that you won't have to keep entering the verification text. We should note that while you can use the Google Keyword Tool, Long Tail Pro/Platinum is much quicker and allows you to filter searches, which combined with it's competition analysis make it a worthy purchase.

The keyword tool itself is very easy to use, and very easy to get false information from if you don't know how to use it! You see, Google allows you to search via "Broad Match", "Phrase Match" and "Exact Match". We won't go into detail about the differences here (you can easily Google this yourself), but suffice to say, please only use exact match. It shows you how many people search for the exact phrase that you type in, so it gives you a much better result than either broad or phrase match will. Please note that when you hit the search button, the results will sometimes default to "Ad group ideas", simply click the "Keyword ideas" tabs to see the results you are looking for.

You can also filter your searches by country, so that you can determine how many people are searching for a specific phrase in that country. This result will be displayed under the "Local Monthly Searches" menu heading in the search results.

For example, we did a search for "door handles" in Australia, and it showed that there were approximately 33,100 searches for this key-phrase globally, 2900 of which were in Australia (these figures change over time, so the result you might get from this search may differ).

What you will also notice is that Google gives us a total of 800 keywords that it thinks are related. This is why it is such a magnificent tool, and we think it is one of the eight wonders of the modern world. Here you can find out exactly what people are looking for, how many are looking for it, and where they are looking for it. This is where you find your market.

One factor you should ignore in these results is the "competition" results that it generates. We've lost count of the number of times we've read about people failing to get good search rankings, despite the fact that the competition result was low. This competition result has nothing to do with search engine rankings, it just shows how many advertisers are competing for ad space for that particular keyword, and it is totally irrelevant to you unless you are launching an adwords campaign.

So what should you search for? Anything and everything! If you're trying to brainstorm ideas, go through your local department store and look at products. Write down everything you can think of, and if you couldn't even be bothered doing that, then just spend a few hours browsing on Amazon.com. They pretty much sell everything there is to sell, so it can be a great source of ideas as well. Remember, all you need is one keyword to put into the Google Keyword Tool, and it will spit out 799 others for you to look at as well.

Other factors you may want to consider while looking for a market are:

- There may be a lot of searches for Elephant cages, but can you store and ship them from your garage? Probably not. Keep size and logistics in mind. Don't rule products out just because they might seem to big to ship. Successful businesses are those that overcome problems that others aren't willing to;

- Are you able to source the product cost effectively? We'll go into more depth with product sourcing later, but this is something to keep in mind;

- How fierce is the competition? Again, we'll go more into how to judge your online competition later in this book, but you can use your "common sense" filter initially to cross items like iPhones and iPads off your list;

- Can you brand the item? Being able to add your own branding to the product is a fantastic way to increase your margins. If it's already branded, it introduces sourcing problems, competition issues, and it's not something we would normally touch.

- Is it a product that will cause legal issues? We avoid food products, or any products that may have extensive regulations attached (medical, firearms etc.).

Make sure that the keyword searches you are entering are "product focused". This means that there can't be any doubt that the searcher is looking for that physical product. If someone is searching for "door handles", it's pretty likely they're looking for door handles to purchase. If they're typing in "making your own wooden door handles" then it's pretty clear that this isn't a market you can sell to, unless you are selling a how-to guide.

Some readers may be asking the question, could you seriously build a whole online business around selling branded door handles? Well, it depends very much on your competition, but the concept of selling a very specific object like door handles online (easy to source, brand, ship) as its own business, is absolutely the kind of product we want. Make no mistake, you will not be able to compete with eBay or Amazon when it comes to cheap door handles online, so don't try. What you would be selling are exclusive, branded door handles at anywhere from 2-10 times the price of what you see on Amazon/eBay. We will go into how this is possible later, but for the purposes of this chapter, you just need to understand that a complete online business of your dreams may be selling something as mundane as door handles, and nothing else.

Our focus for each of our online businesses is to have one primary product (based on keyword and competition research), with one or two ancillary products (also based on keyword and competition research, usually with lower traffic than the primary product). The ancillary products are used as additional traffic generators, as well as to increase the average order size through complementary cross-selling techniques. In the door knob example, an ancillary product might be specialised screws for door handles, or perhaps a special screwdriver.

So how much traffic should you be looking for? We generally look for products that have a local search volume (we focus on local searches, as they are easier to rank), of at least 1000 exact match searches per month, and the complementary products should have at least 400 exact match searches per month. This is just a guide though, and we have successful businesses with less search volume, and we've also managed to rank well with keywords that have significantly higher search volume. It all depends on the....

...Competition

First of all, you WANT competition. If there is no competition, then there probably isn't a viable market. What you want though, is weak competition. But before we discuss that, let's first talk about how to determine who your main competitors are in the first place.

The number one source of traffic that we receive is from the big "G". Google will become your best friend, and occasionally your worst enemy, but whether you like them or not, this is where the traffic is at. We will discuss other sources of traffic (like social media, PPC, comparison shopping etc.) later in this book, but the overwhelming majority of our traffic comes from Google search results.

I still read "experts" online, who are telling people that to determine your search engine competition, you enter your keyword in quotes into Google, and the number of pages the results return is how big your competition is. This is absolute rubbish, and always has been. Ask yourself, when you last looked for information or a product in Google, how many results did you actually look at? How many pages of Google did you search through? One? Two? Three? The reality is, it is irrelevant how many pages Google has indexed for that keyword, the only competition you should care about are those on page one, and even then, you should be gunning for the top three relevant results. I say relevant, because sometimes Google will throw in a Wikipedia (or other obviously information only website) result, and if someone is actually searching to buy the product, they won't be buying from Wikipedia anytime soon.

So now you can see your actual competition, you need to determine whether or not your site can outrank theirs for your primary keywords. There is no absolute magical formula for working this out, but we have some pretty good guidelines for you to follow to give your business the best chance of success. We can't do this though, without first having some idea of how Google ranks websites.

The real answer to this is that nobody really knows, and as soon as someone figures it out, Google releases an update that changes everything anyway. There are some constant factors though, that are important to understand.

If someone types in "door handles", Google wants to do everything in its considerable power to return the most relevant results to the searcher. It does this by looking at your site, and determining whether or not (based on the content, and even the locality of your site) it will be relevant to the searcher for a particular keyword. It looks at what your site is about by reading the content, and also determines how quickly your site loads among many other factors. It's also a popularity contest. If Google "hears" about your site on other websites (particularly websites that are also relevant to the keyword), and sees that there are people discussing your website in social media, then it figures you must be a popular site. If you are both extremely relevant to the keyword, and very popular, then you are most likely to be able to assist the searcher in what they are looking for, so Google will give you high rankings.

Another key factor that Google loves is longevity. So many online businesses popup and drop off every day, that if Google sees you're around after a few years, then you must be doing something right. This factor is hard for us to surmount with a new site (unless you buy an established site off someone else, which is outside of the scope of this book), but is important to remember that online businesses can easily take a few years to fully "mature".

So relevancy, popularity and age are some key factors in determining a site's rankings, and this is what you look for when trying to judge the strength of your competition.

Relevancy

When looking for how relevant your competition is in Google's eyes, you can use a bit of common sense (is the content all about the keyword you're targeting?), but there are also a couple of quick and dirty ways as well. The number one relevancy key that we look for is the site's page titles. Google loves well optimised page titles, but they also show you what the site owner is targeting as well. If (for example) your competition don't include the primary keyword in their home page title, then it is very likely that their site is not optimised for that keyword. If they are targeting that keyword, but still don't include it in their title (or include a dozen other keywords as well), then it shows that their site is poorly optimised, but Google can't find anything better to put high in the rankings. This, for you, is a great sign, because you won't make that mistake.

Page Rank

Google assigns what is called "Page Rank" to every site, and this is supposed to give you an idea of what level of importance Google gives to that site. While it doesn't give you any particular idea of relevancy to your keyword, if you're competitors' sites are all page rank 5 or above, and include relevant content and titling, then forget competing with them (we will discuss tools for checking page rank at the end of this chapter). We generally look for keywords where the competition has page ranks of 2 or below, but we will compete with higher page ranks if they aren't relevant.

Popularity

One of the age-old tests of a site's "popularity" is by seeing how many other sites are linking to the primary site. These links are known as backlinks. While there are a number of tools that will give you an idea of how many backlinks a particular competitor's site has, it is very difficult to determine the quality of the backlinks. A site that has 10 backlinks from extremely popular and powerful sites (with high Page Rank), can rank a lot higher than a site that has 10,000 backlinks from poor quality sites. For this reason, when trying to judge the competition, we look for competitors' sites to have less than 100 backlinks to the page that is ranking for the keyword (not always the homepage), and ideally less than 10. This way even if the competition has high quality links, you should still be able to knock them off over time. If you're using a tool like Long Tail Pro/Platinum, it will not only give you an idea of how many backlinks a particular competitor has, but also how many of these links are actually quality links (known as "Juice Page Links").

Age

While age is an important factor, we tend not to worry about it too much when judging the competition. If the competition passes our previous tests, then we know we can beat them regardless of how long they've been around.

To a lot of SEO (Search Engine Optimisation) gurus out there, this will all seem a bit too simple. They will explain that there are millions of factors that go into SEO, and that you need to pay a lot of money to get a real competition analysis done. This is absolutely true if you are trying to enter a highly competitive market. The whole point of this business model is that we want to find the very low hanging fruit out there, and then walk in with our ninja skills and dominate the search as quickly as possible.

So how do we find these things out quickly? There are plenty of free tools (check out SEO Quake toolbar at seoquake.com), but we use Long Tail Platinum (http://www.longtailpro.com/) for competition analysis. It finds the top ten sites, and will display Page Rank, Age, and backlinks for each site, as well is Domain Authority, Page Authority and its own metric – Keyword Competition (KC).

KC (Long Tail Pro/Platinum Keyword Competition Metric)

A relatively new competition metric we are using is the "Keyword Competition" metric in Long Tail Platinum. While the developers of the software don't reveal the secret sauce that goes into this metric, they developed it as a way to measure how relevant a particular page is to a given keyword.

For example, there are metrics out there (like page rank or page authority) that give you an idea of how authoritative the page is, but this is pretty generalised, and doesn't necessarily mean that it will be hard for you to beat that site. You might have a few page rank four or five sites in your top ten competition, but if they aren't well optimised for the particular keyword you're looking at, then it might still be easy for you to rank. Long Tail Platinum will give you a KC for each page in your top ten competition results, as well as an average KC for the top ten. We look for keywords where the top ten results have an average KC of less than 35, but ideally less than 30. The lower the better!

Searching for the right keyword/market/product can actually be quite fun. You may find yourself getting a bit disillusioned though once you start doing competition analysis and find that the amazing keywords you keep finding have intense competition. You might even find yourself wondering if you can bend some of the competition rules slightly because you particularly like Product A and it has lots of searches. Here's what will happen if you do:

You will follow the rest of the book to the letter, and purchase your products, build your website, and then pay for ongoing marketing and SEO. After 2-3 years of not getting any decent search engine rankings, you'll probably walk away from the business, having wasted a lot of time and money, and missing out on other opportunities. You might think I'm sounding a bit harsh, but you've got to understand that spending a few weeks getting exactly the right market, with very low competition, can save you years of heartache and a lot of money. There are companies out there who spend hundreds of thousands of dollars per year on search engine optimisation alone, and unless you're willing to do the same, you will not be able to compete. But if you choose the right market now, in a few years time you'll be the one that nobody wants to compete with, because you will have the right site, years of SEO behind the site, and Google longevity as well. So please be diligent, be patient, don't settle for anything less than the diamond in the rough. There are a near infinite number of products out there, with new products being created every single day, you just might have to dig a bit to find them.

Give yourself a set period of time – at least a week – and try to come up with as many "winners" as you can. While it's possible that the first one that meets the criteria will be the one you run with, it's good to have a number of keywords that meet the criteria, as this will allow you to choose the cream of the crop, and also give you some keywords to fall back on in case you have difficulty with product sourcing for your primary.

Ebay Completed Listings

Another way to confirm your market, is to look at similar products on eBay. After you log in to ebay, it will also allow you to filter the search results by "Completed Listings". This will then show you how many products sold, how many didn't sell, and what prices items sold for. Don't get too disheartened if you see a lot of unsold listings, or low selling prices. Ebay is a very saturated market for most items, and the margins are very small. We don't put too much value in this method any more, as the previous method is a lot more indicative of success, but we still mention it because it will give you a good indication of what styles of product are selling. If we use our door handles example, searching on eBay might show that people are buying more designer door handles than your standard generic handles, so this can help influence what samples you initially purchase.

Do I Need To Be Passionate About The Product?

Definitely not. It can help, but can also hinder your decision-making process. This is because you really want it to work, as it's something that you love. This doesn't mean that you shouldn't run with the product just because you are passionate about it, but you should be careful and make doubly sure that you don't cut corners. Forget the passion, is there enough traffic? Is the competition weak enough? These boring pieces of data will be your closest friends.

You will no doubt have read books that say you must be passionate about your product for your business to succeed. This is a great line that makes people feel warm and fuzzy about running their own shop, but it isn't true. There are multi-gazillion dollar businesses out there selling the most mundane of products, that are doing very well thanks very much. That doesn't mean there isn't room for passion in your business (you SHOULD be passionate about changing your life), but that doesn't have to flow through to your product choice.

One of the first stories I read about online retail (before we got started) was about a lady who had become a millionaire by selling spa parts on eBay. She wasn't passionate about spa parts, but strangely enough, she was passionate about the million dollars.

Our Story

"When we first started, we didn't know about the Google keyword tool, how to judge our competition effectively, or many of the other concepts listed here. We had eBay and that was about it. Our first business (now vurgejewellery.com), is probably not one that we would start today, despite the fact that it is still going and still successful.

We actually started with a couple of different products (including cigar humidors!), and only four different ring styles in only three sizes! It took us years to get vurgejewellery.com to the point where it is getting a good level of consistent relevant traffic every day, whereas using the tips we've discussed in this chapter, you can reach the same levels in 6-12 months, and in some cases we've done it in 8-12 weeks."

"Takeaway Tips"

- Find a market before worrying about finding a product;

- Make sure the market is large enough to be worthwhile;

- Only enter a market that has low competition on page one of Google;

- Check out eBay's completed listings.

Still have questions about where to start, or how to find a product to sell? Feel free to ask us at www.talknbusiness.com.

Chapter 3 - Product Sourcing

So you've done your research, and decided that you are going to launch www.doorhandles.com. There's only one problem – you have no idea where to buy door handles from. Do not pass go, do not collect $200, just go straight to www.alibaba.com. Here you will find suppliers from all over the world vying to get your business. "This is amazing" you say, as you start to learn that for $0.99c per piece, you can buy the same door handle that your local retailer sells for $19.99. Sure you have to buy 1000pcs per style, but think of the profit margin! You can sell them for half the price as the local retailer, and soon you'll be sipping Pina Coladas on an island in Thailand (highly recommended by the way).

Of course, it doesn't work like that, even though this seems to be the approach a lot of people seem to take. While we do source most of our products through suppliers that are on Alibaba, we have learnt to take a different approach than what we did when we started our first online business. This is where we need to introduce the concept of the "minimum viable product".

There are many factors that will determine whether or not your business is successful, and as much as we try to minimise risk, you can never totally get rid of it, particularly at the startup stage. Until you have sales coming in, you do not know whether or not this business will be successful. That is why we want you to "scale in" to the business with "minimum viable product". This means that you want to spend as little money as possible in getting a website up with product that people can purchase, and still get value out of. In other words, don't worry about spending squillions of dollars on the fancy packaging just yet, and maybe the designs you're getting in aren't exactly part of your long term plan, and maybe you're paying just a bit more per item than you would be willing to in future just so that you don't have to buy as much product for now. This obviously means you are spending a lot less money on your setup, but has the distinct drawback of not quite being the business that you envisage for the future. The problem is, you don't really have any idea whether or not your dream business will actually be viable yet. If you're an online business, you don't quite know whether you'll get the rankings you want until you get them, or be able to achieve the traffic levels you'll need to become a viable business, so the idea is to spend as little as possible until you do know.

All of the research you have done in the previous chapter will not 100% guarantee a viable business. There is no research in the world that can do that, all you can do is maximise your chances by using the methods contained in the previous chapter, and then spend as little as possible until you know that you have a winner. The internet is the only place I know where you can open a store, and wait for the customers to start coming in before spending money on any product.

The reason we are focusing on this in the product sourcing chapter, is that this is where your costs can quickly spiral out of control. You're so excited about finding that keyword, and all of a sudden in your mind's eye you can see this amazing looking, professionally developed and customised website with the most amazing and largest range of tap handles on the planet, and anything less than your vision simply will not do. You start to justify this to yourself by saying things like "If I build it they will come", or "Google will love me if I have the biggest range". I'm not saying that to have that vision is wrong, I'm just saying that you should build up to that level. Scale in and manage the risk along the way.

We actually build a site, get content on it, and wait till it starts ranking before we buy any product at all, even samples. This is because with our experience we know whether or not we'll be able to source the product once the traffic starts coming in. We don't put "fake" products on the site, we make it very clear that we have no products in stock, and that they are "coming soon" products. Once the traffic starts rolling in, then we start getting the initial range in small quantities to start testing conversion.

So how do you do this when suppliers want massive quantities per product? Well, first of all, they are usually highly negotiable, but often not enough to get it down to one piece per model. This is where we have learnt some great tips over the years, and if you remember nothing else from this book, then please remember these:

- Ask for samples. Say that you are looking for a new supplier, and are getting samples from a few companies to check the quality. This is the ideal scenario, because if a few suppliers say yes, then not only will you have a start up range of products, but when you do start getting good traffic to your site, you'll know which suppliers have the best service/product/delivery times etc. Some of the drawbacks can be that they'll want you to pay a "sample fee", or alternatively want you to pay ten times the price for the item. Don't do this, as it defeats the purpose of keeping things cheap. Feel free to contact a hundred suppliers if you can, it costs nothing to ask;

- Ask if they have any items in stock. Manufacturers often do overruns, or have customers that didn't pay, and they are left with stock on hand that they can't get rid of. This is a great way of getting low quantities of perfectly good stock;

- Ask if they currently have any orders you can piggyback onto. If they have a large customer that is ordering at the required minimum order quantity, sometimes a supplier will make an extra one or two at the same time which you can purchase. This method is more easily done when you have an established relationship with the supplier;

- Use Aliexpress.com. This version of Alibaba is where suppliers try to move some of their in stock items at low quantities. It's a great place to get an initial range;

- Buy from eBay. It may sound odd to you that you can go and buy from a site on eBay and then sell it on your website but it is very possible and is done all the time. Ebay is branded (whether they like it or not) as a garage sale style place to buy cheap goods. Even if you brand your listings well, it is difficult to achieve good prices on eBay in our experience. We started our business on eBay, but found that a product we couldn't sell for more than $30-40 on eBay could be sold on a well placed, well branded website for over $150. While we wouldn't use eBay as a steady source of supply for your business, it's a great way to get some initial stock.

We like to start with about 25-50 different SKUs (stock keeping units), which we source using any/all of the methods above. This gives you a full looking website, that can be well optimised for Google, as well as looking like a real business for any customer that arrives. You can also start your comparison shopping and social media campaigns based on this site.

Should I Source Locally Or Overseas?

That's entirely up to you. If you live in a western nation, you may find it difficult to find a local manufacturer of, well, anything. If you do find a local manufacturer of the product you wish to sell, you may be shocked at the price differential, even with shipping costs. On rare occasions though, you may find a local manufacturer that has close to the same prices as overseas manufacturers, in which case this can be a great asset to your business, so long as you are still getting great service and quality products. Being able to advertise that you use a local manufacturer can be a great marketing tool.

In general though, you will probably find that local manufacturers simply cannot compete with the overseas competition.

How To Pay For The Product

Making those first few transfers overseas can be extremely daunting, but they're nothing to lose sleep over. There are only two methods of payment we ever use, and they are T/T (Telegraphic Transfer) and PayPal. T/Ts can be made either online through your bank, or at your local branch, and aren't all that different from making a normal transfer. Make sure you have the recipient's correct address (both company and bank branch), and swift code. The chances are that they will have already sent this to you in the invoice. We've only had one problem with T/T, and that's when I put the wrong address in the transfer details and the supplier never received the funds. I simply rang the bank, explained the problem, and within 24 hours the funds were back in my account. T/Ts do come with a cost though, which vary from bank to bank, which is why we find it more cost effective to use PayPal for transfers under $1000, while we use T/T for transfers above $1000.

PayPal usually finds in favour of the purchaser in any payment dispute, so we use them as much as possible.

Shipping

How you ship your product back to your warehouse (yes, even if your warehouse is your lounge room or garage) will depend on both where you source your product from, and the size and quantity of the product. As the vast majority of products you will be looking at are small and sourced overseas, this can be a source of confusion and fear for someone who hasn't done this before.

Until you have your business well and truly up and running (and probably more than one), it's still cost effective, and far less hassle, to use companies like DHL, TNT and FedEx. If you choose to ship via sea, it will not only take much longer, but you will normally have to deal with customs on the other end, as well as dealing with another freight company if you can't get to customs yourself. We've tried to go down this path before, and not only was it slower, but it ended up costing us just as much (if not more), and also took a few years off our lives.

Shipping via one of the express carriers will not only get your product to you much more quickly, but they take care of the customs side of things for you, and will see the product delivered directly to your door.

One BIG tip we'd like you to walk away with is to let your supplier use their shipping accounts, or at least do a split test for yourself. We were quite burnt with some of these major carriers, because we were using our own accounts. What this means is that instead of the supplier charging us for shipping, we would give them our account number, and then the courier company would charge us later for the shipping. We recently did an experiment from the same supplier, for the same size/weight package. Using the supplier's account (in China), the shipping cost $35USD. Using our account ended up costing us a whopping $100USD, for exactly the same package! Needless to say, we hope this tip saves you a lot of money.

A Final Word On Product Sourcing

What we want you to take away from this is that organising shipping/customs from an overseas supplier doesn't need to be scary or daunting. We've used 30+ suppliers over the years, and have had very few problems at all. If you receive broken or damaged merchandise, take a photo and get back to them as quickly as possible. Often the supplier will ask you to send the items back for credit/refund, just like a western supplier might – ask them for their shipping account number so that they pay for the return shipment (we have done this successfully, but they won't always do it).

You will have the occasional problem, and will get the odd bad supplier who sends you rubbish and takes your money. If you're using somewhere like eBay or Alibaba.com, make sure you report them, and leave them negative feedback where possible. The reason why we always get samples, and always start with multiple suppliers is because it significantly lowers your risk. We've seen and heard of several people losing thousands of dollars because they go "all in" on one supplier who they've never used before! You're in control, so exercise that control. If a supplier won't do a sample, or they are going to charge you a 10x sample fee, then it doesn't matter how pretty their catalogue is, or how cheap their prices are, walk away.

Finally, we want you to "smile" when dealing with suppliers. When you're negotiating in just about any culture, it's really important to stay friendly throughout the negotiation, even if you feel they are being unreasonable. The idea being that both parties can "save face" even if they are unable to come to agreeable terms. Emailing your suppliers should be done in the same manner. Once you have found a great supplier, and you are negotiating prices and quantities, you need to be extra friendly, as they can make your life very easy or very difficult, depending on your relationship. Emailing is very impersonal, and it's easy for both parties to misread a situation, especially if English isn't someone's first language. Be nice, and you will get better terms.

Our Story

"Looking back at our biggest mistakes in product sourcing, I'd have to say that we didn't get enough samples, and we spent way too much money on stock. We didn't negotiate well, and we didn't realise how much power was in our hands. Initially, suppliers would tell us that we had to order as many as 200pcs per size/style for our rings, whereas today we have ways of regularly getting only 1pc per size/style. Let me tell you, that makes for a far more efficient business!

There was another time where we had to throw out hundreds of items due to poor quality, which could have been avoided. Not because we didn't order enough samples (this was from a supplier we had used several times before with great quality), but because we didn't negotiate well enough to get smaller quantities in the first place. This demonstrated to us that not only do smaller quantities help from a capital expenditure perspective, but also from a risk management perspective.

While you should definitely build a great relationship with your suppliers, if they can't do what you need them to do, you need to look elsewhere. We had a great supplier (who treated us to an amazing feast when we visited them in China) that unfortunately just could not provide the range or prices that we needed if we were to continue to grow. It was difficult to leave them, but we needed to make sure that the business didn't suffer just because we had a great relationship"

"Takeaway Tips"

- Contact as many potential suppliers as you can;

- Order samples or over-runs from at least 3 different suppliers;

- Build your initial range from these samples;

- Use Telegraphic Transfer or PayPal for payment;

- Use the supplier's shipping account.

Still have questions about sourcing product? Feel free to ask us at www.talknbusiness.com.

Chapter 4 - Building Your Website

There are many options out there for selling a product where you don't even need a website (eg. Ebay, Amazon, Facebook stores). In our experience though, building your own branded website allows you to sell your product at a premium, and also allows you to build better relationships with your customers.

The first thing you need to do is purchase a domain name, which means you need to name your business. Google recently publicly stated that having your keywords in your domain name won't provide as much benefit in the future as it has in the past, which while it may sound negative, is still an admission that Google gives some benefit to having your keywords in the domain name. From our perspective, we try to do this if it makes sense, but don't place too much emphasis on it. In our door handles example, it might make sense to call your business www.doorhandlesonline.com, if the domain name is available. Having the primary keyword in the domain name is not a bad idea (not just for SEO purposes) as it tells your customer exactly what your business sells as well. Google also loves local. If you want to create an International door handle empire, then be my guest, but if you are in Australia for example, you will find it much easier (and cheaper) to rank a .com.au domain name than a .com, and it will make more sense to your Australian customers. This of course assumes that the local search volume is there, and the competition is weak. There are many popular websites where you can register your domain name, but we use godaddy.com.

So given that most of us aren't programmers or designers, where do you start with building your website? There are four main options available to you, a "shopping cart in a box", a site built on an open source shopping cart platform, a fully customised site built just for you, or a free e-commerce solution based on the Wordpress platform. Let's tackle the first three, and ten move on to our current favourite.

A Shopping Cart In A Box

These solutions are where you pay a monthly fee (and sometimes a setup fee) to use someone else's shopping cart solution that is hosted on their site. Shopify, Yahoo Stores and Ashop are all examples of this type of website.

Advantages

-Minimal startup fees;
-When they roll out new upgrades, they're normally included.

Disadvantages

-Never as customisable as you want;
-Ongoing cost adds up over time to become more expensive than other solutions;
-Can sometimes make changes that you don't want, and there is nothing you can do about it;
-Every time you want to start a new business, you have to pay another monthly   fee.

Open Source Platform

There are large communities out there who together have developed bare bones e-commerce systems that you are allowed to setup and customise (or have customised) to your heart's content, all for nothing. Examples include Zen Cart, OsCommerce and Magento.

Advantages

-Usually quite customisable;
-A community who creates new features for you;
-Easy to find developers to add features or make design changes cheaply;
-Easy to have replicated for future online businesses.

Disadvantages

-Requires an initial cost to develop the site;
-You need to know a bit more about SEO and design principles to help guide the development.

Fully Customised Website.

When we first looked to have a fully bespoke site built by Australian web design firms, the quotes came in at between $30,000-$100,000. We chose not to use them.

Advantages

-Totally customised to the way you want it;

Disadvantages

-Normally quite costly, both to build, to maintain, and to make any changes.

Wordpress + Woocommerce

While we have used all of the previously mentioned platforms, at the start of 2013 we started to more seriously explore the option of using Wordpress (the world's most popular stand alone blogging platform) combined with the free e-commerce plugin Woocommerce. While we had visited this option in the past without as much success as we'd hoped, the developers have kept developing (as good developers do), and what they have come up with is amazing and frustrating at the same time.

Frustrating because with the right theme, setup and plugins, a free Wordpress site with a $60 theme and a few free plugins can do everything our other platform (that has cost us thousands over the years) can do, and a whole lot more. What makes it amazing is that now we can recommend a platform that will not only cost you very little to start with, can be replicated for even less (so you can start multiple sites very cheaply), includes a highly integrated content platform, as well as advanced features like responsive design (your sites will look great on any device, regardless of screen size - from desktops to smartphones).

What we really want to try to get across though, is how important this development is for those who have not started an e-commerce site before, and don't have a lot of money to spare. The ability to start several sites at once, without having the often significant development fees a new platform entails, or even without the ongoing fees a hosted service has, is amazing. This allows you to experiment and try to rank for a few niches right from the word go, without risking a lot of capital in the process.

One of the important steps to take when building a site like this is to choose the right theme. While we'd love to be able to recommend a free theme to use, there aren't any that we've found that we'd use ourselves. One of the best places to find themes is at www.themeforest.com, where you can just do a search for "woocommerce", and it will show you a range of different themes that will be suitable. We personally use the Mayashop theme, and can certainly recommend it.

The Drawbacks

Of course nothing is perfect, and neither is Woo-commerce. There will always be certain features that we'd like to have but are a bit more restricted. Having said that, you can always find a developer to help code those extra features if you need to (unlike hosted solutions), although we haven't found that necessary as yet. One major feature we'd like to see is better support for those of us that manage a large number of stores, but it's something we're happy to sacrifice in return for the other benefits that it brings.

The other drawback is that while Wordpress, and most of the plugins involved are free, you'll still need to set it up. While I'm sure that there are plenty of people out there who would be happy to relieve you of some money to do it for you, we'd rather show you how ourselves, as this will allow you to get to know the system, and also save you money as you grow your portfolio. It's not easy to do this in a book, so we've created a video where you can see us building an example site in a series of workshops you can find at www.talknbusiness.com. Please keep in mind that much of the process that you will see is based on using the Mayashop theme (a link is provided below the video), and other themes will need to be setup differently.

So which solution is best for you?

We personally have used the first two solutions and the last solution in our journey, and still can't see the point of the third solution for this style of business. Starting off with a hosted solution can be a cheap way of testing the market (we used Ashop, but others like BigCommerce.com are cheaper and seem to have a good reputation), but we became too frustrated with the customisation restrictions to use long term, and as soon as you decide to launch a second (third, fourth...) site it becomes very costly. For example, a typical cart-in-a-box solution may set you back $25-100 per month per site, whereas our current hosting costs us $7 per month, with no additional ongoing costs (some carts charge a per transaction fee as well). So you can see, if you have 5 online businesses, at $7 per month, you would be paying $35 per month total, whereas if they were using a hosted solution, you could be up for easily as much as $500 per month, for something that isn't as good. That's a massive difference!

So how much should it cost you to setup a customised site based on an open source solution? Well, the costs can obviously vary, but the same site that would have cost us $30,000-$100,000 ended up costing us about $2,500 for an OsCommerce based solution developed by a company in India (through elance.com). This was with all of our specifications, with the design based around a couple of award winning sites that we liked.

This was a good solution, but still kept draining our pockets for continuous changes over the years. We've now moved all of our sites across to the Wordpress solution, and are experiencing better rankings, better conversions and longer time spent on site. In addition, we can also change the look of each site quite dramatically.

The other benefit is that new plugins and themes are released for Wordpress all the time that will help improve the your sites even more, and most of them are free. It's a great solution, particularly when you are following our model of creating multiple sites.

Hosting

For the non-hosted options, you will need to organise hosting yourself. This is where another company stores your website files so that other people can view it. Hosting these days can be very cheap, or very expensive depending on where you host, and what options you would like.

There are a number of providers out there who believe that if you are going to target Australian consumers (for example), you will get much better rankings in Google's local search if your site is hosted in Australia. This hasn't been our experience, and we have no problems with hosting overseas, where we get better service, up-time and price, without any noticeable sacrifice in speed or rankings. Specifically, we use Hostgator.com, who have a well deserved excellent reputation. You don't need to get a "business plan" or "enterprise plan" or anything crazy, just one of the basic plans will do. If one of your sites becomes a runaway success, you may want to consider upgrading, but stick with one of the low cost plans until that happens.

Should You Have A Mobile Site?

We made the commitment that when 10% of our visitors were mobile shoppers that we'd add mobile sites to our existing sites. We hit this level early this year, and so we made the move. As mentioned, we were able to do this very cost effectively, and would recommend you do the same. We still wouldn't consider it to be absolutely vital yet though, as visitors are still able to view your products with a normal site. With the staggering rate of growth in this area, it's hard not to see having a mobile site as anything but necessary going forward, but if you're cash strapped, this is one added cost that you can add in later.

If you decide to use the Wordpress solution, and choose a responsive theme (like the Mayashop theme we use), then this is no longer an issue, as your site will automatically re-size and reconfigure itself to be useable according to the screen size being used. Magic!

Product Photography

Another exceptionally important part of your website is having great product images. This can make or break an online business, and we can't stress how important they are. Fortunately these days good quality digital cameras are found in most households, and buying lighting from eBay is also more cost effective than ever before. If you are going to sell smaller items, investing in a light tent can also be very beneficial. You can usually find complete object photography kits on eBay.

You can touch up the photographs yourself if you need to (using programs like Photoshop, or the free alternative "Gimp"), or you can outsource this (learn how to outsource in later chapters).

Analytics

Having some form of analytics installed in your website is a must. There are some great free options including Google Analytis and Statcounter.com, one of these is all you need. These system then allow you to log in and really track what your website visitors are doing. How many are checking out your site, how many pages they're looking at, what pages they're looking at, what page they came to your website on, the last page they looked at before they left, how long they spent on the site, what page they came from to get to your site, what keywords they used to search for your site, and the list goes on! Once your site is up and running, and you are getting traffic, it's great to really get to know how to use whichever analytics program you run with. The information you get here will help you optimise your site to achieve the best conversion rate you can.

Currently we use Statcounter.com, but we have also used Google Analytics with great success.

Our Story

"Wow, when we look back over the years, we have had quite a few ups and downs when it comes to our selling platforms. We initially were ripped off by a company that took our money but never provided a website. At the same time we were selling on eBay, a platform that while it was a great place to start, has an awful lot of issues for sellers. We were paying up to $8000 per month in eBay fees alone, just to sell on a platform that due to its very nature forces you to sell at a discount.

We used multichannel systems that cost hundreds of dollars a month that had great auction site integration, but terrible e-commerce platforms, and moved to a shopping cart in a box platform that then cost $100 per month.

We then developed our own open source based e-commerce site, that cost about $7 a month to run, and was really good., but we did start to get a bit frustrated at the difficulty with getting it to work on mobile devices, so decided to trial the Wordpress+Woocommerce+Mayashop solution. This ended up being yet another improvement again, and we wish it was available when we first started as it would have saved us thousands of dollars!"

"Takeaway Tips"

- Start with a hosted solution and scale up when you're making money;

- Take great photos of your product (or find someone who can!);

- Use analytics to find out how many people are visiting your site (and what they're doing once they get there).

Still have questions about building your website? Feel free to ask us at www.talknbusiness.com.

Chapter 5 - Building A Traffic Machine

Natural Search Engine Traffic

"Build it and they will come" a great quote from someone who never tried to succeed in online retail. One of the reasons why we want you to start with a minimum viable product strategy, is because we put "natural qualified traffic" above all else. Of course, you need to have a site up with product to be able to get that traffic in the first place, but you don't need hundreds of SKUs, or fancy packaging to do so.

So what exactly is "natural qualified traffic"? These are consumers who are looking to buy the kinds of products that you are selling, but that you didn't have to pay for. We still believe in some paid traffic options, but the holy grail is getting the traffic for free. There are some other places to get free qualified traffic (eg. Social Networking) but while these don't necessarily cost you money, they do cost time. Easy enough to outsource, but then they're costing you money!

So once again we're back to the big 'G'. Getting traffic through Google (not Google paid ads) is still the best way to get consistent, free, qualified traffic through your virtual doors. One of the fun parts about having an online business though, is that you have hundreds, maybe thousands of doors you don't even know about yet. While the majority of searchers will use the primary keywords, there are almost as many people who type in phrases you couldn't even think of. You'll find that people come to your site by typing in "stainless silver handle for walnut doors" or some phrase that's barely legible. They're still free, still qualified, but these phrases aren't used enough to register for Google's Keyword Tool, and you'll make plenty of sales just the same.

These have become known as "Longtail Keywords" and are some of your best friends. They're also why you can and should be a little descriptive in your product page titles.

So let's talk about getting your site ranked. There are two expressions you will need to become familiar with – on-page optimisation and off-page optimisation. On-page optimisation refers to the factors on your website that will help you rank better, and off-page optimisation refers to off-site factors that affect your rankings.

On Page Optimisation

It goes without saying that your content (home page, helpful articles, product pages) needs to be about your given keyword. Once upon a time, you could just "stuff" your website full of the keyword you wanted to rank for, and that was all you needed to do. These days you need to be careful if your keyword density get's above 2%. For our purposes, you just need to make sure that all of your content on your site is natural. We don't get too hung up on specific densities, we just make sure that the article is relevant to the topic, and that the topic is relevant to the keywords we'd like to rank for. What we consider to be a bit more important is making sure that the titles of all of your pages are optimised, and that relevant headings are also used.

If you are targeting the keyword "door handles", because it get's 10 times more searches than door knobs, then make sure that for each of your products, the phrase "door handles" is used. Don't overdo it (eg. Don't make the title of all of your pages "Door Handles"), but use additional adjectives to mix it up a bit (eg. "Stainless Steel Door Handle, "Gold Door Handle", "Antique Door Handle", "Red Door Handle"). This will also help you get a whole lot of those wonderful longtail keywords we discussed previously. If you are using a website that titles your pages by the product's model number or SKU, then you definitely need to get that fixed.

You should also make sure that your URLs are relevant. For example, if you use an open source shopping cart system (eg. OsCommerce, Magento etc.) you might find that by default your products' URL's look a bit like this:

http://www.mysite.com/product_info.php?products_id=258.

This is bad, and you really want them to look like this instead:

http://www.mysite.com/red-door-handle/

So make sure your designer knows this before you get your website built. If you forget though, it isn't costly to get fixed, and in our opinion is absolutely vital to the success of the site.

Off Page Optimisation

This can be where things get a little trickier. Technically, Google doesn't want you to build any "fake" links to your site, and any off site links should be other websites naturally talking about you. Nor does it like you to swap links with other sites, and nor does it like you paying for links. The problem (as we see it) is that there are always methods of getting links back to your site that will boost your rankings, that Google doesn't know about. This puts website owners in a quandary. Either you do exactly what Google wants (but you go out of business because your competitors have a better link building strategy), or you do something Google doesn't want you to do, and go out and build links for the purpose of ranking higher.

Link Building is a tricky subject, as nobody knows exactly what will work at any given time. It can also be fraught with danger, as we found out the hard way. We had an SEO contractor that used to build links for our site, and this boosted our sites in the rankings. When Google started playing "bad cop" in 2012, some of our new sites were penalised hard. This meant that they dropped out of the rankings completely. Our SEO company didn't believe it was their fault, so we had to go about proving that it was. To do this, we setup brand new sites in the same niches, then started conducting experiments of our own. Sure enough, we had those sites ranking within months, while the original sites weren't even in the top 500 for their keywords. Needless to say, we don't use that company anymore! It also forced us to rethink our off page SEO strategy.

We decided to conduct a range of different experiments, which included four new SEO contractors/companies, as well as conducting our our personal strategy. We built four sites with very similar traffic and competition, and got started. Please note, SEO can take a long time to prove its success, so it could be a while before this experiment will truly be complete. Keep an eye on www.talknbusiness.com for the final results. We've included it here to give you an idea of what is possible.

Contractor 1

This contractor we found through www.warriorforum.com, who had great testimonials, and charged $50 for link-building until your site reaches page one. This contractor managed to get the site penalised so badly that I doubt we'll ever see it again. Experiment complete.

Contractor 2

Contractor 2 we found through elance.com, an outsroucing site. We posted a job that offered $250USD to any contractor who could rank our site to page one for its primary keyword, but they would only received payment once the site reached page one. Effectively, this means the contractor would be working for free until they achieved success. We did find a contractor willing to do this, and at the time of writing their site is almost to page one for not only its primary keyword, but several others as well. Needless to say we've been pretty happy with this contractor!

Contractor 3

We advertised on Odesk.com for a contractor who could get our site to page one for its primary keyword. We had no luck finding a pay for performance contractor, but found one that seemed to have previous success, who charged $100USD per month. After a couple of months of seeing a lot less success than contractor 2, and with no end in sight for how much we'd end up paying him (after all, the longer he takes, the more he get's paid...), we cancelled the contract.

Contractor 4

This was another pay for performance contractor from elance.com. We couldn't quite negotiate the terms to be as good as contractor 2, but at the time, we had no real idea whether or not contractor 2 would be any good, so we thought we'd better have a backup. The terms were as follows:

- They would be paid $100 once the site hit the top 50 for its primary search term;
- They would be paid an additional $100 once the site hit the top 20;
- They would be paid a final payment of $150 once the site hit page one.

At the time of writing, the site has hit the top 50, but has dropped back to the "60s".

Our SEO

Soon after beginning these experiments, we decided to do our own as well. We started a brand new site, added great content, and got started with backlinking.

The premise behind our strategy was to only do relevant linking, using original helpful content (where content was required) and ensuring that we only "add" to the internet experience. You have to remember that we were still pretty burnt at this stage by having so many sites penalised, so we were going to tread very carefully.

Directories

Our first step was to submit the site to about 20 business directories. There are a lot of bad "spam" directories out there, so we went and found all of the top human edited business directories in Australia (which is where we want the site to rank) and submitted the site, with unique descriptions. Each of these directory profiles contained a link back to our site.

Google Local / Places

We also submitted the site to Google Local / Places. This is Google's way of proving that you are a real business, and they will verify your business address by sending you out a postcard with a code on it.

Social Media

We then opened accounts for the site on Facebook, Pinterest, Twitter and Google Plus. All of these accounts allow links back to your site, and also tell Google that you are serious about allowing your customers to interact with you in the manner of their choosing.

Squidoo

Squidoo is a community where you can create a "lens", which is kind of like a single page website. These lenses seem to have a bit of authority with Google, so we created one the centered around our topic (good, helpful, well written content that would add to the community – not spam it), and included a couple of links back to our site.

Tumblr.com, Wordpress.com, Blogger.com, LiveJournal.com

These free to use blogging sites are also communities that you can add to. We created a blog on each of these platforms. Again, all of these blogs have original, helpful, well written content that would be useful to someone interested on the topic. Each blog also included two links back to our site.

Forum Posts

We also found forums that were related to our niche, and participated in conversations with helpful, insightful commentary, and included a link back to our site in the signature. One the keys to this strategy is getting on the first page of the conversation. When somebody starts a "conversation" on a forum, other people respond (usually) and the conversation can carry through to several pages, and in some cases, for hundreds of pages. The first page of any forum conversation always carries a lot more weight than subsequent pages, so you want to be getting on board either early on, or for conversations that are only one page long.

Blog Comments

Like forum posts, we also found blogs and blog posts that were related to our niche, and commented with a link back to our site. Again, if you don't provided helpful comments that relate directly to the blog post, your comment will almost certainly be deleted by the blog moderator, so make your comments count.

That's it! The only ongoing backlinking we're doing is ongoing blog comments at this stage, and the site is outperforming all of the contractors, and is at the top of page two for two of its primary keywords after a massive 12 days of backlinking.

Summary

As you can see, we're pretty happy with both the results of at least one of our contractors, as well as our own results. I both cases, we record every link that is made back to our site (the contractor provides a report every week), and this is really important. Never use a contractor that won't deliver this report, because if they start giving you bad links, Google now has a way for you to "disavow" those links, so long as you know where they are. If you don't know, and you are penalised, you often have to start again from scratch.

You will also notice a pattern in how we managed to get our links. With the directories, they're all really business directories that are run by real people that review every submission. This benefits searchers who use directories, as well as searchers who are looking for our contact information. The Squidoo lens and blogs are original, helpful sources of information that also add to the internet experience rather than spam it. The blog comments and forum posts help other and also add to the overall internet experience, not just for you but for others as well. All of the techniques we describe here are abused more often than used to add value to the internet. Your success will be determined by how well you use them, not by the mediums themselves.

Finally

One of the reasons these methods work for us and work relatively quickly, is due to the fact that we chose low competition niches and products to start with. If you have chosen a harder niche, expect to have to do exponentially more work, and for it to take a lot longer.

SEO is also not a science. The internet is full of forums filled with "experts" arguing over what works and what doesn't, and some of them would argue until they're blue in the face that what we've talked about doesn't work. These are not arguments we'd get involved in, as we're too busy using the aforementioned techniques to rank our sites, multiple times, with great success. We believe that a lot of the arguments stem from different people trying to use the same techniques to rank medium to high competition sites, and when it doesn't work, they lay the blame on the wrong aspect of their business.

Content

In addition to the above forms of on page and off page SEO, we also do a bit of content producing ourselves. It's important that when Google checks your site, it finds great content, and we believe that should extend beyond just your product information pages. One of the worst things about content is constantly creating it, one of the best things is that it can be re-purposed in quite a few different ways.

One of the reasons you'll see a blog on many retail sites, is not because lots of people want to read a blog about door handles, but because they are a great way to add content to a retail site without that content getting in the way of conversions. The articles might be about latest products, product specifications, "how to" articles for proper use of your products, or the pros and cons of different types of products. It's easy enough to install a basic Wordpress blog in a subdirectory of your website (eg. http://www.mysite.com/blog), and add an article every week or two. If you run with the Wordpress + WooCommerce option like we have, then your site will integrate content better and easier still. In every article, we recommend creating two links to "deep" pages on your website. For example, if the text "door handles" was found in one of your articles, instead of linking that text back to your homepage, link it to either a product or category page instead. We'll talk about how to outsource article creation later, but for now we can discuss how to turn your article into a...

...YouTube Video

Another way to drive traffic to your website is through online video, predominantly YouTube.com. There are a number of ways to create video content, not all of which require a video camera. One of the most cost effective ways to put up some good videos is to create presentations from your articles that give customers more information about your product.

You can either create the presentations yourself (using Microsoft Powerpoint or the free Open Office Impress), or outsource it, although we'd recommend learning how to do a few yourself, so that you can give an example of what you want to potential contractors. They're quite simple to do, and very effective.

To turn these into videos, we use another free program call CamStudio. It simply captures everything on your desktop and turns it into a video. So all you need to do then is hit the record button in

CamStudio, and run your presentation. You can either do a voice-over, or add a free (and royalty free) music track afterward. Once the video is complete, you can upload the video to YouTube.

A couple of things to note here, please ensure that you include your website url at the bottom of every slide of your presentation, and turn this into a hyperlink. While this won't be a clickable link when you turn into into a video, it will be when you...

A Final Word On Content

Google is all about good quality content, so it's important that you deliver this to them. One of the temptations with content is to produce something that's quick but a bit "light" on actual content, or to outsource it as cheaply as possible and get something barely readable. Google is pretty good at reading English these days, and will only get better with time. We personally think you are better off releasing one good quality article per fortnight than one poor quality article per week. Content is becoming more an more important as time goes by, particularly with all of the change Google has made recently.

Outsourcing Content Production

Producing content can be both time consuming and draining at times, and once you have a few sites, it can be difficult to keep it up. Outsourcing content production is way to keep the level of content on your sites increasing, but it can be fraught with danger.

We have outsourced content many times, with some successes and some failures. It's so tempting to let mistakes and grammar issues go, but it's vitally important to make sure that the content is written very well (for natural English readers), and is also helpful in some way. This content represents your brand, and if it is poorly written, it will reflect poorly on your product offering.

We outsource much of our content now, and do so through

Odesk.com. Our content is helpful, well written, and costs us about $3.30USD per 500 words. The reason we are able to get it done this cheaply, is because we worked hard to find someone who could write like a native English speaker, and gave them bulk articles to do. If you give someone only one article at a time, expect it to cost several times more to get good quality. We also go through every article thoroughly as it comes in to make sure it fits our standards.

Pay Per Click Advertising

To PPC Or Not To PPC... That Is The Question.

Pay per click advertising like Google Adwords or Facebook ads can certainly be a quick way of getting targeted traffic to your site. But is it still a viable method? To be honest, we don't use them anymore, and here's why. They're just too expensive, and we have patience. The only reason we would use them at all would be to test the viability of a business model quickly. The problem here is that our online retail businesses are built with two major forms of traffic in mind, natural Google traffic and social networking traffic primarily through Facebook and Pinterest. While you can definitely find search volumes for your keywords, and do a reasonably thorough SEO analysis of current competition, there is still no absolutely foolproof way of knowing whether or not you'll be able to cost effectively rank a site for any given keyword. The only way to really find out is to get your site up (with a minimum viable product strategy), and slowly start building your search engine presence. We usually give a site 6-12 months before we make a decision about whether or not we can crack the top five in Google search results for its primary keywords. The other benefit of doing this is that you'll start to find out how many longtail keywords there are driving traffic to your site. Sometimes you won't even need to crack Google for your primary keywords, as you can often get enough traffic just from the longtails to make a business viable.

So the problem with PPC is that even if you spend lots of money to get traffic to prove that your website can convert, it still gives you no indication as to whether or not you'll ever be able to get decent natural search traffic. If you can pay for these ads, and still make a decent profit off the traffic, then by all means please do so, but don't do it at a loss in the belief that you've now "proven" your business model, and that you will be profitable once you get the rankings. Online retail (and any business) is a game that requires patience. Don't overestimate what you can achieve in the short term (with PPC), but by the same token, don't underestimate what you can achieve in the long term (through social and natural search).

Comparison Shopping

Comparison shopping sites like Bizrate, Nextag, Get Price, and others, are sites that allow you to advertise your products alongside other advertisers. The benefit is that the consumer can compare similar products from a range of websites all in the one spot. These are actually PPC models in that you (the advertiser) don't normally pay until somebody clicks through to your site.

The reason we have kept them separate from more traditional forms of PPC like adwords and Facebook Ads, is that we actually use them! Sure they cost money, but the difference is that the customer has seen the specific product, and its price (and often your shipping and returns policies) *before* they click through to your site. This results in a much higher conversion rate than someone who has seen a tiny text ad. A word of caution though, do your research on every comparison site before signing up. Some have exorbitantly high click-through costs (depending on category), and others require a minimum number of SKUs to be advertised, otherwise they charge a large setup fee.

To be honest, we don't get a lot of sales from comparison shopping sites, but we get enough to make it worthwhile. The comparison sites will ask you for a "product feed". This is a spreadsheet that contains all of your product data, and most website systems can export feeds (and if it's an open source platform, often there will be contributions that will export the feed). Alternatively, you can manually produce one as well using any spreadsheet program. All of the comparison sites that we have dealt with have had someone to guide you through the process, so don't be afraid to keep contacting them.

Social Media

Social networking platforms like Facebook and Twitter have often been cited as the new "must have" sources of traffic. There is no question they can be very useful, but how you use them can be dependent on what kind of business you have. The very nature of social networking also means that you have to be very careful about how you approach each platform as a business or sales tool. As an online retail business, the last thing you should do is bombard your fans with incessant sales pitches, but you need to constantly keep their attention. So how do you go about doing this? Each platform is different, so we will guide you through each one separately.

Facebook

Facebook is our favorite social media network to start out on. Why? Well it is kind of like a shop window for your customers, they can see others interacting with your brand, plus they can learn about your product in an environment that is already comfortable to them. Did you know that over 250 million people log into Facebook daily? That is a lot of potential customers for your new brand. If you already have a personal Facebook page than starting a business page will not seem like a big task. There are plenty of guides online that will help you set it up, but here is how we approach getting it ready to promote your business:

Starting A Facebook Business Page:

- Create a Facebook business page;

- Add all your business details. Don't forget the "about you" part, people want to know who you are and why you exist. Why do people want to be a fan of your brand?;

- Add your cover photo, this is the long image at the top of your Facebook page. There are particular rules with this image, such as no branding/selling or requesting likes;

- Add a profile picture. A logo or person works well, something clear that people will be able to recognise amongst all of their notifications;

- Now you want to make your page feel alive, lived in by your customers. To do this you can:

- Add a post. This is a small portion of text on your page wall. Not all of your fans will be able to see your post thanks to new Facebook rules, but you still need to post;

- Create some tabs. A great tab to create first is "contact me" so that customers can get in touch. We use a website called "Shortstack" to create our tabs. This is free up until you reach a certain amount of fans. You can find out more at www.shortstack.com;

- Add a photo album. People want to see your product, and you should categorise them like you would on your website. You do not want your entire collection of product in one album. Also make sure your categories make sense and are easy to use;

- Get at least 25 fans as quickly as possible through ladders*, inviting friends and family and adding a link on your website.

- Make your Facebook url your business name. This can not be done until you hit the 25 fan mark, thus the above step! Your Facebook URL will look like www.facebook.com/yoursitename. If you're not sure how to do this yet, do a search for "facebook username" or "facebook vanity URL";

- Make a posting plan that will provide regular stimulus to your fans. We have an excel document with quotes, jokes, images and a whole bunch of product related tips. We then pick one a day. We post using an 80/20 principle....80% of the posts are fun and non-selling and the other 20% are a deal or product related.

*ladders are where several businesses work together to "like" each others' pages. This can be a quick method of getting a few fans. You can find ladder pages by completing a search for 'ladders' or 'tagging' in Facebook's search bar.

Once you get this system going, you'll find it much easier to create a Facebook presence for each of your businesses. Being able to systemise the interaction is the key to staying on top of social media, and sticking to the 80/20 posting rule is a must. You can't just sell sell sell. You also need to be on the lookout for customer questions and comments, and respond to them as quickly as possible.

Twitter

Twitter is a slightly different animal. If you haven't used it before, it essentially allows you to post short pieces of text that other people can follow. Facebook very kindly allows you to link your business fan page to a twitter account. This means that every time you post to Facebook, it automatically posts to Twitter as well. Genius! However, you can tweet many tips for followers throughout the day, unlike Facebook where you should limit your posts to 1 or 2 a day. The easiest way to stay motivated and on track with Twitter tips is to create a database of Twitter tips that customers following your brand would find helpful, and then mark them off as you post them. As you get to learn the best time to tweet for your brand and the style of tips, you can schedule your tweets with the use of free programs such as FutureTweets.

Pinterest

Pinterest may be the new kid on the social media block, but it's causing quite a stir, particularly among online retailers like us. Pinterest is an image-based social media platform where users can surf the web, "pinning" images to their Pinterest board so that they can go back to their board later and see what they like.

Imagine someone surfing the web looking for a yellow scarf. They go to numerous online retail stores, each of which has a scarf that may or may not be a winner. They "pin" each one to their board, as well as a few photos of celebrities wearing yellow scarves (because they're so hot right now), and then go back to their board so that they can make a decision.

That example should make it pretty clear that you will need to get involved with Pinterest, but there are other ways to use Pinterest to promote your site as well. Like the other social media platforms, you first need to create an account. To do this you need to request an invite from Pinterest and wait for them to accept you. When setting up your account, do not use the "automatically create my account using my Facebook page". This will link it to your personal Facebook page, and you want to create your own so that you can name it after your business. Pinterest does not have a business name option, only a first name and surname, so split your business name if it has two or more words. Once you've done this, you can create "boards" which you can then pin images to. This allows you and your customers to categorise images. Follow other Pinterest boards that are relevant, this way you will have fresh content to re-pin and they may just follow you back. It is really important that you pin original content as well. Original content from your website will not only promote your product, but it will create backlinks to your website. Others that click on your original pins will be taken to your website, thus driving traffic.

Your pins should always contain a description and key words that will help people find your pins, for example, if a person searches for a yellow scarf and your description of a yellow scarf only contained the words "This is the winner, I love it", then it won't come up in the search. This may not seem like a problem, but if you want people to find what you are selling, it has to contain the key words. Another great thing to do is include the price. The price will then appear across your image and will come up in Pinterest's Gift section.

Social Media On Your Website

Make sure that you use social media on your website as well. This means adding social buttons that allow people to "like" your website or products, or "pin" your products onto their Pinterest board. You should also have a link to your social media presence on every page of your website (eg. a link to your Facebook Fan Page). Having a social media presence will make customers feel as though they are not alone on your website, it will feel like a busy and buzzing store which ultimately leads to greater sales. Using code from somewhere like addthis.com is fairly easy to do and pretty straightforward.

The Best Form Of Traffic

For all of the benefits an additional traffic avenues like social media, PPC and Comparison Shopping can bring, even when combined they pale in comparison to the traffic and sales that Google natural search can bring to your site. We can certainly understand though that nobody wants to be totally reliant on one form of traffic, but when it comes to getting a business going, Google is where it's at.

There is another form of traffic that will keep your business going (and growing), regardless of your current Google rank, and that's repeat and referral traffic. Much of our business comes from either customers who have already purchased from us before, or from their friends and family. The only way to get this kind of traffic is to truly please your customers, and give them a great experience from start to finish. There are also tools that can assist you like "ShareYourCart" (free and easy to integrate into Wordpress+WooCommerce as well as other hosted solutions) that allow you to give your customers a small discount during checkout on the condition that they share their purchase with their friends on social media. At the end of the day though, nothing beats great customer service, a great product, and great branding.

A Final Word On Traffic

Good quality traffic takes time to build. We're not talking weeks here, we're talking months. You really have to be patient, and follow through on everything you've just read in this chapter. While that may sound easy enough now, wait until you've been writing content every week, paying SEO companies to build links, paying for your website, trying to get fans for Facebook, pinning like crazy, running competitions and sending out emails to your one subscriber who has an email address called "neveropenmyemails@gmail.com". It can get really discouraging. Now that we've done this several times, we know that there is usually (not always) a light at the end of the tunnel, but when you are first starting out, you don't even know if the tunnel ever ends. You must be patient, and you must be diligent. You need to focus on the end game, and why you started this in the first place, as this is what will get you through.

Once that traffic does start coming in, and you realise that these are real people, searching for the actual products that you're selling, then it's time to get excited! At least until you start wondering why nobody is actually buying anything.

Our Story

"How to crack the search engines is always the top conversation among website owners, but it has not been of the greatest concern to us lately. This is because we build sites that Google wants, and doesn't have enough of. I truly feel sorry for online business owners who have spent a lot of time and money on websites that are in highly competitive markets. Even if you have the budget to fight off the constant competition, you will need to sustain this budget for the life of the business. There are still so many untapped markets out there with little to no competition, that it doesn't make sense to enter the blood soaked waters of highly competitive markets.

The focus of our first successful online business has always been wedding rings. But we would never enter this market again, simply because the traffic levels aren't there for such a highly competitive market. We have been successful, and will continue to grow this business, but it has taken years to do as well as we have, and it will probably take another few years to get it to where we really want it.

We don't want you to have to wait that long. It will still take time, but if you choose the right low competition market, cracking the search engine rankings doesn't have to be expensive or time consuming."

"Takeaway Tips"

- Google is king, get your on page optimisation right first;

- Use the Warrior Forum to find an off page SEO provider (with great testimonials and repeat customers);

- Build great content into your site;

- "Repurpose" content into Youtube videos and slideshows;

- Use cost effective comparison shopping sites;

- Use Facebook, Twitter and Pinterest to create communities that will drive more traffic and conversions for your business.

Still have questions about driving traffic to your site? Feel free to ask us at www.talknbusiness.com.

Chapter 6 - Conversion

Once you are getting the traffic to your site, it's time to think about converting some of it to sales. If you are already getting sales, great! But there's always room for improvement. There are a number of ways to do this, so let's address them in turn.

Pricing

Getting the pricing of your products right requires experimentation. It's natural to want to discount your prices when the sales aren't coming in, but you must try everything else in your arsenal before doing this, as it can dramatically affect the profitability of your business, and it may not be the problem in the first place. Consider these two scenarios:

Scenario A:

You purchase door handles for $5 each
You sell 10 door handles per week for $30 each

Scenario B:

You purchase door handles for $5 each
You sell 50 door handles per week for $10 each

I can tell you which scenario would feel more successful. Scenario B means you're moving 5 times the product, receiving much higher revenue, and it would feel like product is racing out the door! Some of the more mathematically minded readers might be saying wait, I can see what you've done, 10 sales at $25 profit in Scenario A results in $250 gross profit, while 50 sales at $5 profit in Scenario B also results in $250 gross profit, so both the scenarios have the same result.

Anyone who's run a successful business though, might be saying that Scenario A is so much better in reality than Scenario B it's not funny. Why? Because although both scenarios result in the same gross profit, Scenario B has five times the logistical issues, five times the customer complaints, five times the supplier issues – five times the problems (and associated costs) for only the same gross profit. You can bet your bottom dollar than Scenario A is putting the greater *net* profit in the bank every week, and that the owner is sleeping much better at night.

There is a reason why Louis Vuitton can sell handbags for $3000, and yet remain in business for far longer than the thousands of discount handbag stores that have come and gone.

As previously mentioned, going discount online means you will be competing with the likes of Amazon and eBay, and you won't win. What you need to do is be an upper market online specialty store. Customers will still expect you to be cheaper than equivalent offline bricks and mortar stores (they are not silly, they know you aren't paying the same rent and costs, and expect some of that to show through to your prices), but it's okay to charge more, so long as you are providing more perceived value than the large online discount stores.

So how do you achieve this? Well, the very fact that you have a whole business dedicated to door handles is a good start! You become the expert in door handles. You provide articles on how to install different types of door handles. What are the latest trends in door handles for modern homes. Which door handles are practical, and which ones are purely about design. What are the benefits of steel door handles and what are the drawbacks of gold plated door handles? Hopefully you are starting to get the picture. If visitors to your site instantly get the feeling that nobody knows door handles like you know door handles, then subconsciously they will allow for a greater price premium.

You make sure that you have clear exchange and return policies, and at least a 100% money back satisfaction guarantee. Some studies have shown that 110% money back guarantees significantly increase conversion rates, yet very few people will ever utilise the policy. In the same vein of thought, you could offer lifetime guarantees, or even a 100 year guarantee. It shows you believe in your product, and while you will have the occasional return, it just turns into a numbers game after a while, and you will figure out whether or not it's worth it to you.

What you can do if you're really worried that your price is too high, is to have a sale for a month. You can discount the price this way without permanently reducing them. If you find that conversions increase dramatically, and you are still very profitable (do your maths and work out the net profit, remembering our Scenario A and B example from before), then you can consider a permanent change. Just remember, it is far easier to reduce prices than it is to raise them.

Site Design

Site design is also a big factor in conversion, and seems to be an ever changing landscape. Once upon a time you were supposed to have a big red "Add to Cart" button on your product pages so that people would know which button to click to purchase the product. These days studies have shown that everyone knows now what "Add to cart" means, and that red can be considered to be too high pressure, and can turn a customer off (apparently blue or green are the colours of today).

But while some aspects change, some stay the same.

Do:

- offer multiple payment options
- only have 2-3 clicks to checkout
- make product filtering easy
- have a clear, single page checkout

Don't:

- force customers to register before purchasing
- use lots of flash
- make customers have to wait for slow loading images
- distract the customer with too many bright flashing ads or offers

Product Range And Mix

Once you start getting traffic, you can then start to think about spending more money on product. The beauty of waiting for traffic before expanding your product range, is that often you can look through your traffic statistics and find out some of the longtail keyword searches that are bringing people to your site. You might find for example, that more people come to your site via the search phrase "stainless steel door handles" than any other specific type. This of course means that now when you order product, you might want to get some more stainless steel door handle designs!

One problem in offline retail stores is the lack of space. Customers say they want more choice, but when presented with a lot of choice in a physical environment, they often freeze, and end up not buying anything. Online is different, because you can filter out options very easily. That's not a licence to go out and spend your life savings on the largest range of door handles in existence, but ultimately you do want to be the expert in door handles, and be able to serve the customer whatever they are looking for. As a caveat, the rule of "too much choice" still applies. Once someone has narrowed their choice down to "Door Handles → Designer → Stainless Steel" (with only two clicks at most), you don't want to give them a hundred different options, keep it down to no more than a page or two ideally.

Payment Types

Five years ago, you couldn't just have PayPal as an option, as it gave your site the reputation of being a bit "cheap". These days, PayPal is much more mainstream, and if you don't offer it, then you have a problem. This is a good thing for small to medium sized websites, as merchant facilities can be very costly, and from our experience don't add as much value as they used to. PayPal allows customers to pay from their PayPal account, or if they don't have one, they can also pay directly via a range of credit cards. We offer PayPal and Bank Deposit (popular in Australia), but make sure to advertise VISA and Mastercard as well, even though it is also processed through PayPal.

We still see articles where business magazines will say that you "must" have another merchant account besides PayPal, and that it will increase your conversion rate. We haven't seen this to be the case, and the exorbitant cost (at least in Australia) of opening and maintaining a merchant facility far outweighs any conversion benefit that we have seen.

Email Newsletter

Having customers or visitors subscribe to an email newsletter is also still a good conversion technique. Studies have shown that the average person usually comes into contact with your brand 6-7 times before feeling comfortable with purchasing from you, so adding an extra few contacts via email is always a good thing. Keep in mind though that they know you are a retail outlet, and typically they expect some sort of occasional discount in exchange for their details. We don't mind this form of discount, because they're not getting it for free. They are allowing you to regularly contact them, which can result in more than one purchase over time, which makes up for the discounting. You can also advertise sales of slow moving items, and let them know about your latest article on "Keeping Your Door Handles Shiny".

We use mailchimp.com, as they have a great free option for low volume users, which is exactly what you'll be at first. They are also easy to setup, have good support, and will cost-effectively scale with your business.

Phone Support

Should you advertise a contact number on your website? We'd advise that you try it and see if it helps improve your conversion rate. If it doesn't, then you may not need it. We've tried normal phone numbers, 1800 free numbers, and no phone number, and we no longer use a phone number at all. When we had a phone number, we found that we would get a call maybe once every two or three weeks, and this was normally a support issue, not a conversion issue. It could be argued though that the very presence of a phone number may increase your conversion rate as customers feel "safer" purchasing from a website that advertises a contact number. This is something that is worth split testing, but from our perspective, we prefer to answer as many questions as possible in the website content itself, then make contact via email or social media super easy for the client. Depending on the lifestyle that you're trying to create, even if a phone number increases your conversion rate by 10%, it may not be worth the extra hassle.

As a caveat though, if you don't have a phone number, make sure that emails are being responded to very quickly. Less than 24 hours is the usual metric, but customers love it when you can respond either instantly, or at least very quickly.

Our Story

"One of the hardest things I had to come to grips with when entering the retail game for the first time was pricing. It took me years to learn what the word "value" really means to other people, and how to provide it. The best way I came to terms with a product's value proposition was to change my definition of what our product was. Instead of looking at a wedding ring as the product for example, I had to start looking at the product as being what the customer experienced.

When we originally sent out rings, they were through eBay (among a bunch of other seller's listings), with no returns policies, in a plastic wrap in an envelope. Now we sell through a boutique branded website (with social community), we offer a lifetime guarantee, full free exchange policies, and when the customer receives their ring, it's in a full branded modern ring box, with gold foiled warranty cards (with shipping date for easy reference), and a free ring sizer that can help them with future purchases, or if they need to change the size.

So our "product" has evolved greatly over time, and so has our price. Don't be afraid to raise your price, but be sure to add value when you do."

Takeaway Tips

- Be competitive with pricing, but don't be too cheap;

- Make sure shoppers can easily navigate your site and proceed to checkout;

- Don't force customers to register on your site before they can checkout;

- Monitor your traffic to determine what products you should be focusing on in future;

- Use email newsletters to help increase conversion over time.

Still have questions about converting more customers? Feel free to ask us at www.talknbusiness.com.

Chapter 7 - Shipping & Logistics

Shipping

This is a hard subject to deal with for an international audience, as the shipping options vary so wildly from country to country. What we would suggest is that you contact your local post office as well as every courier company you can. You will be surprised at the wild variations between costs. One courier company will charge you $100 to ship your item to a destination, while another will only charge $5, this seems too crazy to be true, but believe us when we say it happens.

Every six months, we'd also suggest you review your shipping costs, and recontact courier companies to see what has changed.

The same goes for the question "should you ship internationally". If it makes sense financially to do so, then by all means do it. We have shipped to over 50 different countries, and have had no major problems doing this at all. What we did find is that our Post Office would ship our smaller items anywhere in the world for $1.80 so long as they fit through a cardboard "slot" that they had behind the counter. If it didn't fall through the slot, then it would cost $10.80 instead. Of course, it also depended on who was behind the counter, and whether or not they had had a good night's sleep or not!

All you can do is research the options you have available. What we wouldn't do is become too reliant on overseas trade. At one point, we were selling more product to international customers than Australians, then the exchange rate changed dramatically, and all of a sudden our products "doubled in price" for our international customers, and we immediately changed our focus back to our domestic market.

Warehousing

In the spirit of keeping your costs minimal until you start making good money, keep your product at home! Nobody will know that your "warehouse" is actually a spare room or a garage, and nor will anybody care. Keep a clear area separate from your household goods, and always refer to it as your "warehouse". Sure your friends and family might scoff at you for doing this, but it's important to remember what the area is for. Keep it secure, and make sure you have all packing and shipping materials within easy reach and in stock. In fact, we would even go so far to suggest you get a sign made up with your business or company name logo to put on the wall. Give yourself and others no doubt about what the area is for. Later on this will help make sure that employees/contractors who come into your warehouse know that they are coming into a designated work area, which will help inspire them to do a better job, and treat your business as a real one.

The other reason we'd suggest doing this, is that it will make it easier when you start contracting someone to come and do the shipping for you. Getting a real warehouse somewhere may impress your friends, but can cost an absolute fortune, and is an unnecessary cost at the beginning, and indeed for a long time.

Be sure to check your local zoning laws though, as while it's usually okay to run a business from home, residential zoning can have restrictions on how many employees can work there, and how many times trucks/vans can turn up to your property. We hire a large double garage from someone who doesn't use it (in a residential zone), and are allowed to have 2 employees working there at once. This rent costs us about one seventh of renting a separate warehouse in a commercial area, and we'll be keeping our warehouse there as long as we possibly can.

Another option is to use a fulfillment centre. These are businesses that will receive, store and ship your product for you. It's a great concept in theory, and one we hope continues to evolve (Australia is well behind other countries in this regard), but we have just not been able to make this work from a cost/benefit perspective yet.

Our Story

"Our warehousing has evolved from a desk in a two bedroom apartment (that was robbed), to a garden shed the heated up like an oven in summer, to a double garage that has been setup to be a proper warehouse. There has always been the temptation to get a "real" commercial warehouse, but it simply hasn't ever made financial or business sense to do so. Your friends and family may (or may not) think that you're running a backyard business, but your customers won't know or care – and they're the ones that matter!

We are lucky to have a family member who runs the warehouse for us (and who takes the position very seriously), although we have contracted others in from time to time who have done a good job as well. How you run your warehousing is up to you, but we would still recommend doing it yourself for quite a while, so that you can work out your systems.

Getting someone to run your warehouse (or even just work in it) is a big responsibility. You really need someone you can trust who will take the position seriously. This is a real business you are starting, and you need to impress that upon whoever works in it."

"Takeaway Tips"

- Ship it yourself to start with;

- Do your research, as shipping/courier companies can vary greatly;

- Set aside a specific, dedicated area for your "warehouse";

- If you start employing help, make sure you abide by your local zoning laws.

Still have questions about warehousing and logistics? Feel free to ask us at www.talknbusiness.com.

Chapter 8 - Branding

What Is Branding?

There are many different definitions of branding out there, so we might as well add ours to the list! Your brand is the impression that your customers come away with any time they come into contact with your business.

By this definition, the more you excel in website design, customer support, and shipping, the better your brand will be, and the more you can charge for your products/services. On the flip side, you can have beautiful logos and website design, and excellent customer service, but if the customer receives their item much later than they expected, your brand will suffer in their eyes. You can also have an excellent product, excellent customer service, and fast shipping, but if your website and logo come across as being a bit "cheap", then your brand suffers.

Branding goes beyond just making your customers feel good though. Great branding is where you make your customers feel what you want them to feel. You guide their emotions. Even the price you charge is part of your branding strategy. Many people (if not most) believe that if they pay more for a product, it must be better than a similar product being sold for a lower price. It took us years before we raised our prices for one business and when we finally did we not only raised them, we tripled them. Guess what? Not only did our sales not plummet, we started making more money than we did before. We've even heard of businesses who tripled their prices, and then watched in amazement as their sales quadrupled, as customers then had a greater perceived value for their products. This sounds weird, but if you think about it, a customer doesn't want to feel like they bought a "cheap" item. They certainly don't want their friends to think that, so by raising your prices, you're giving them what they want.

We've mentioned previously in this book that we don't want you to try and compete in the same space as Amazon or eBay. These guys are the kings of cheap pricing, and you will never compete with them, so don't try. What you are going to offer is a more premium, branded experience. You don't buy a cheap door handle off eBay because you think the eBay seller is a door handle expert. You buy it because you want the cheapest door handle you can buy, and hope that the quality is good enough to last a year or two. People don't ask eBay sellers what they recommend in a stainless steel door handle design either, because this is not why people go to eBay.

There are many, many customers out there who want more from their purchasing experience than an eBay seller can provide. They want to feel like they bought from a specialist, they want to pay a higher price (they'll never tell you that, and never admit it, but it's absolutely true), and they want to be able to tell everyone where they bought the item from. "I bought it from eBay" does not give them bragging rights. We're not saying there is anything wrong with eBay at all, we're just saying that their customers will not be your customers.

Our Story

"Being able to brand your business and your products is the key to setting your business apart from the likes of Amazon and eBay, so it's vital that you take it seriously. If you're not gifted with Graphic Design skills, be sure to outsource your logo and website design to someone who can do them professionally. This doesn't need to cost a fortune either, as you can use places like fiverr.com, elance.com and odesk.com.

Your branding also includes your interaction with customers. We have completely outsourced our customer support before, with varying degrees of success. Whenever we are building new businesses though, we always do it ourselves for a while. This allows us to develop FAQs and standard responses, so that our brand doesn't suffer when we hand over the reigns to outsiders.

One customer support representative we had was really good to start with, so we stopped monitoring his responses. After a while though we started hearing about some issues, we started checking a few customer responses, and found out that this representative had stopped using the standard responses file we'd given them, and was now giving our customers completely false information.

Your brand is what will allow you to charge higher prices, get repeat business, and spread word of mouth about your business. So be sure to protect it!"

"Takeaway Tips"

- Branding is making your customers feel what you want them to;

- Make sure your policies and website match your pricing;

- Don't be scared to raise your prices, but add "perceived value" as you do so;

- Give great customer service!

Still have questions about branding your website? Feel free to ask us at www.talknbusiness.com.

Chapter 9 - Empire Building

While this book has so far specifically addressed the research and launching of one site, it's really important to consider launching more than one. We'd recommend sticking with one until it's profitable and ticking along nicely, but having several sites bringing in income has a lot of benefits. The obvious one is more money! Not only that, but you will also have fixed costs like storage, internet and a range of other costs that don't change regardless of how many sites you have.

One of the main risks associated with online retail is that no matter how many comparison sites you're on, or how active you are in social media, the majority of great traffic comes from Google. Once you have those search engine rankings that you've worked so hard to achieve, it can be really unsettling when Google does a major update, and your site loses rankings for a week or two. There are also some pretty scary stories out there about good, solid, very profitable sites going broke after a single Google update. The moral of the story is, Google is a great friend, and also your greatest risk. There is little you can do about this, except diversify. If you have ten sites, and you lose a couple in a Google shake-up, you haven't lost all of your income. I've even heard about sites disappearing, then popping right back up to where they were a year later (which is usually because of a Google penalty)! If you have other sites to get you through, then you have the opportunity to be patient.

Once you've built your initial website (that's your own, not a hosted solution) you can also duplicate it for a fraction of the initial building cost, and then any upgrade costs are shared across all of your businesses.

The more businesses you have, the more product you're moving. Economies of scale mean that it will now be easier to negotiate better shipping costs, and it also becomes more cost effective to employ someone to do the shipping for you, or to use a fulfillment centre.

It also becomes more viable to employ or contract someone to take care of your customer service. While initially you handle the questions and issues yourself, over time you develop a "FAQ" (frequently asked questions) that you filter customers through before contacting you. This can dramatically reduce the number of questions you actually receive, which is great, but makes it difficult to contract someone to do your customer support when there is only the occasional question to answer. This might be fine for your situation, but when you're on an island in Thailand and don't have power let alone the internet, you tend to lie awake wondering if you are going to miss out on the sale that will pay for your whole week, just because you weren't able to answer that one question.

Having multiple sites means you can justify contracting someone to check customer questions for all of your businesses, while still costing you very little. Please do not underestimate the value of waking up and having absolutely nothing that you have to do that day. It is a life changing feeling.

Additionally, you may need to build a number of sites to replace your current income. If you spent $4000 over the course of your first year, and the site still only returns $150 per week net profit, you can't retire, but is it a failure? Your ongoing costs are negligible, and $150 per week results in $7800 per year from a $4000 investment. Try getting that return in the stock market. What if you used the Wordpress based ecommerce site, and, but this time it only costs you $1000 due to the fact that you are more experienced and only purchased minimum viable product. Now this site again only returns you $150 per week. That's a $7800 return on a $1000 investment.

Now imagine you have 10 sites, all returning $150 per week... get the picture? In the final chapter, we'll show you how to retire once you hit $300 per week (although this might not be suitable for everyone!). The reality is, we don't have any mature sites that earn that little, but hopefully the illustration serves to highlight my point.

There is also another benefit to creating more than one business, in that you really can create your own little empire. Imagine starting with your door handle business, then creating other sites also related to home interior hardware (tap handles?). You can then link all of the sites, and start cross selling and advertising products that are complementary to your current customer base. This also creates relevant backlinks for Google, and strengthens your company's standing as an expert in a wider field. Excited yet? You should be!

Outsourcing

While we've touched on outsourcing throughout this book, it is a subject that requires more detail. There are several ways to find contractors, but finding a good one is just as difficult as finding a good employee locally.

For customer support, website building, graphic design, and social media support, we find contractors on elance.com and odesk.com. There are other sites out there that I'm sure are just as good, but these are the sites we have used. We tend to use elance.com for projects (eg. Develop a website with these specifications), and odesk.com for hourly jobs (eg. Spend one hour per week pinning images for our Pinterest accounts).

These sites are very easy to use, as all you do is post the project you want, with the conditions and rates that you want, and wait for the contractors to bid. Usually, there are so many offers that there is little point selecting a contractor who has less than 4.5 stars (out of 5), and if you need someone to help with customer support, then they should speak good English. Don't be afraid to trial a few until you get one that suits your needs.

We also use Fiverr.com for small SEO jobs and graphic design/video work. Fiverr.com is where people will do jobs for $5USD and can be a lot of fun to play with. Be warned though, most of the SEO "gigs" on Fiver.com (as in 99%) will at best do nothing for your site, and at worst will get your site penalised. Here are some of the types of "gigs" that we use Fiverr.com for:

- Niche relevant blog commenting
- Niche relevant forum posting
- Logo design
- Banner design
- Squidoo lens creation

Customer support is one of the hardest things to outsource, because customers are very sensitive to dealing with someone who doesn't speak very good English. In our experience, you may be better off paying the extra to get a native English speaker. Alternatively, make sure you have a customer support manual that contains responses to most questions, so that the customer support representative mostly just cuts and pastes the answers as required, only making minor alterations to more directly answer a customer's concerns.

One of the most important aspects of outsourcing, is to make sure you are crystal clear about what you want the contractor to do. Much of the frustration that can eventuate from outsourcing can be alleviated from your end. Your employee/contractor needs very specific instructions, that also include expected outcomes as well as time limits and deadlines.

Make no mistake, outsourcing can be as frustrating as it can be rewarding, but it is both worth it and necessary in the end.

Probably the final frontier of making your online retail empire passive is storage and shipping. As discussed previously, we would suggest initially that you ship the products yourself to reduce costs, but as you grow, you will need to be able to completely outsource this. There are a couple of ways to go about this. Firstly, you can hire someone to do your shipping, even if it is from your garage. Alternatively, you can use a fulfillment company. These are businesses that will receive the product from your suppliers, store it, and then ship it for you when an order comes through. They are definitely a more expensive option, but nowhere near as expensive as renting a warehouse and having staff.

We would recommend contracting a trusted family member or friend to do the shipping as you grow, and once you have a few businesses going, consider moving to a fulfillment centre. The cost of using a fulfillment centre will depend on the size of the products you are selling, as well as how many you are moving.

I Don't Want To Wait, I Want An Empire Now!

This is understandable! For a traditional retail business, you are looking at a bare minimum of $100,000 just to get started, and that would be with a very small store. With our model, you could start 100 businesses for the same cost, dramatically reducing your risk. The problem is, if you haven't successfully launched even one site yet (and it's profitable and passive), any growing issues are magnified by however many sites you do have.

We once were privileged enough to have a mentoring meeting with Don Meij, the multi-millionaire CEO of Dominos Pizza in Australia/New Zealand. When we asked him how we should grow, his response was simple. Make one business profitable, then do it again. Sounds very basic, but as has often been said, business is simple, but never easy. We would encourage you to have patience, and get that first one off the ground and at least paying its own way before starting your next business. At that point, you may be more willing and able to start another two or more at the same time (or eight as we did), but this is partly because you will already have your shipping and logistics setup, your website already developed, you will be an expert in domain names, product sourcing, hosting and everything else in between.

Our Story

"One of the main reasons we started creating multiple businesses was because there wasn't any real way of pushing our original business any faster. Not only that, but we had learnt so much, that we wanted to use our new-found knowledge and experience to create even better businesses.

It was that first business that gave us that experience though, as well as the confidence and income to move forward. This is why we don't recommend starting your empire before having at least one good successful business under your belt. When I look back and wonder what would have happened if we had started our new businesses a year or two earlier, all I can see is how many problems would have been multiplied had we done so.

We not only needed our business to be at a certain level before we could start more, we ourselves also needed to be at a certain level."

"Takeaway Tips"

- First things first, get one profitable business going before starting your second;

- Once the first one is running smoothly, make it as passive as possible;

- Start building more businesses (ideally within the same market as the first website, but not totally necessary);

- Make sure you cross promote between sites if it makes sense to do so.

Still have questions about empire building? Feel free to ask us at www.talknbusiness.com.

Chapter 10 - "So Where Do I Start?"

Now you're excited and rearing to get started, we'd like to give you a word of caution. The one thing you are going to need in bucket loads before you get started is patience. It takes time to find the right product, it takes time to find the right supplier(s) and get samples, it takes time to find the right developer/hosted shopping cart, and most of all, it takes time to build traffic to the site. How long? Well, it varies wildly. We normally give our sites a year before we expect them to make any real income. That's right, a year. It normally doesn't take that long, but some do, and we psychologically prepare ourselves for this eventuality before we go into any project, and you should too. This is actually one of the reasons why we now start a number of sites at once, simply because it gives us something to do!

That's the bad news, but now we want to give you our recommendations for what we would do if we had to start all over again.

What We Would Do

If we were to start all over again, from scratch, we would start with a different attitude, as well as this system. First of all, feel free to be skeptical. There are lots of books and websites telling you how to make money online, and most of them will cost you money and time. We do have a few credentials (we have been invited to and have spoken at online retail conferences and panels, and are often interviewed based on our successes, we are currently running e-commerce businesses, growing new ones, and Tess won the Alibaba.com Female Ambassadorship for 2012 etc.), but it's important to test and measure for yourself before rushing headlong into any business. So start with one site, and you'll know soon enough if what we say has merit, and doesn't just work, but works in today's online environment. The caveat to this is that you have to follow the recipe (all of it), and you have to give it time, otherwise you're not truly testing our system. It may seem simple to do in principle, but it is very easy to gloss over some aspects of the system in your excitement to get going, and you can waste a lot of time, or even worse "prove" to yourself that this system doesn't work, even though you never really gave it a proper go. So with that caution, let's go!

We would start with one site, purchase Longtail Platinum and find the lowest competition niche we could, even if we had to sacrifice traffic to do it (not completely sacrifice though, we'd still want to find a niche with a bare minimum of 2000 local exact match searches amongst its top 3-4 highly related keywords, ideally with its primary keyword having around the 1000 exact match local searches). We'd want to know can we actually rank a site before buying product, so we wouldn't stop looking until we had the lowest competition niche we could find.

I would then head to Aliexpress.com, Alibaba.com and Ebay.com in that order to find out whether or not I can source the product, and get an idea of how much it would cost to source an initial range. Then I would head to my potential competition in the Google top ten results for my primary keyword(s), and see how much they're selling the product for. Now I know what my potential gross profit margin will be, I can get an idea of how profitable the business might be. If you can't sell the product for at least double what you bought it for (including shipping to your "warehouse"), then pass.

Then I'd register a domain name, and get the the cheapest hosting I can from Hostgator.com (I can always upgrade later when I want to add multiple websites). I'd then purchase the Mayashop theme, and install wordpress+woocommerce+Mayashop in accordance with the workshops at www.talknbusiness.com. I wouldn't bother with a logo yet, or a banner, but I'd buy a relevant image for the front page of the site from stockfresh.com.

I would then create a complete keyword map using Longtail Platinum, and once I was sure it was complete, I'd "downgrade" Longtail Platinum to Longtail Pro (saving the $19 per month ongoing fee, you can always upgrade again later if you need to Keyword Competition metric again). I'd then start writing 10-15 articles of 500-1000 words on related topics surrounding the product niche, constantly referring to my keyword map, and add them to the site.

After this, I'd also create product categories and add around 30 "coming soon" products to the site. I'd base these products on similar products found on Aliexpress.com or Ebay.com that could be used to start an initial range when the time comes. I would also add content to the category descriptions, and base the categories where possible from keywords from the keyword map.

Now that my site is somewhat complete, I'd submit it to Google Local / Places, and get it verified, then I'd setup the top four social media accounts as mentioned in this book (and also make sure any new content is automatically posted to Facebook and Twitter). I'd also submit the site to as many "real" business directories as I can, also in accordance with what is mentioned in this book (eg. human reviewed, only "real" businesses allowed)

At this point I'd go register and setup a lens on Squidoo.com, as well as start blogs at Wordpress.com, Tumblr.com, Blogger.com, and LiveJournal.com. I would use original content on each one, articles on helpful, "non-salesy" topics, include images, as well as two links in each that point back to my main site. One of the links would use my primary keyword exactly as its anchor text, while the other link would use either a secondary keyword or more of a phrase match keyword (if the primary keyword is "door handles" my second link might use "designer door handles" as its anchor text instead).

Then I'd be off to find relevant forums and blogs to comment on. Leaving only helpful, useful and relevant comments. I would have links in these comments (if allowed) back to my site. Preferably, 20% of these links would use my primary keyword as the anchor text, with another 20% being phrase match, another 20% being secondary keywords, and the final 40% being random words like "click here" or "check this out", or your name (some blogs will only let you use your name as the link which is fine), or the website URL itself.

I'd do this at a rate of around 20-30 backlinks per week, and keep it going. At this point it's time to "settle in" and keep up forum posts and blog commenting. If you're going to concentrate on one or the another, definitely put more focus on the blog commenting. Remember, both quality and quantity are important, but do not build 100's of these links per week, even if the quality is good.

After a few weeks (sometimes a bit more) I would want to see some movement in the rankings, and I should really start to see my site in the top 100 for its primary keyword. It may dance, it might jump in the rankings and then drop right out, but this is normal, and it will usually settle down. There's really nothing to do but keep up the link building, although if I really had the urge to "do" something, I'd add an article or two to the site itself. I wouldn't really be concerned about whether or not the content is regular, I just would make sure it's well written and on topic, and uses some keywords from the keyword map, without overdoing it.

At some point (often months), my site should reach page one and start climbing. The rank itself doesn't matter so much to me at this stage, I'm more concerned about watching the traffic. Using the analytics I've installed, I'm now watching for the site to start regularly bringing in qualified unique visitors. These visitors may be coming in via my primary keyword, but there's a good chance a few are coming in from highly relevant secondary or longtail keywords. I don't take the analytic's "word" for how many unique visitors are coming to the site either, I go and look at each individual visitor, and make a note of how many are coming in from highly relevant keywords, are from the country I'm targeting, and are clearly "real" people and not automated bots. I'm also taking note of what people are actually searching for (eg. Are they searching for particularl colours, materials or specifications? This information will help guide your initial orders). Once we have a week or two with an average of 10-15 of these real, qualified visitors, then we move on to ordering product.

My preference would be to order products from Aliexpress.com suppliers, who are also able to scale up with my business if needed (so there's a good chance they'll be on Alibaba.com as well). Ideally, you want to be able to order directly through the Aliexpress.com platform, so that you can use their escrow service. I might also ask if they allow factory visits (a great way to find out if they're the actual factory) and ask them if they can provide the full range of designs that they have, as well as minimum order quantities for cheaper pricing. I would then order products from a minimum of three suppliers (unless you absolutely can't find three suitable suppliers, then try Alibaba.com directly and Ebay to find more).

The number of products you'll be ordering will depend on the type of product that you are selling. Some sites we have only sell one product, while others have hundreds. If you are in the "hundreds" category, stick with only getting a total of around 30 for now, 10 from each of your trial suppliers.

I'd also head to fiverr.com and order a logo for the site. I'd check out the designer's previous designs to find something that I like, and tell the designer to give me something similar (but not the same). If the logo didn't work out, they normally will make one revision for free. If I still didn't like it, I'd order from another designer.

I'd also make up a better banner for the homepage of your site. It could still be the same stock image as before, but include some text that should give some reason why people should buy from your site. It could just be something like "Why Settle?" or "Free Shipping", with some text on the front page explaining more.

Once the product comes in, I would check the quality, and see what is in sale-able condition. I would take photos of any defects or problems, and contact the suppliers immediately about rectifying the problem.

For the good product, I'd take photos, and get the product on my site as soon as possible. Id' make sure my descriptions are accurate. I'd also double check and make sure my shipping details and payment options are setup correctly on my website, and make sure that the site is now truly "live".

There's little to do now but wait for that first sale. I wouldn't expect a super conversion rate yet, because I don't know exactly which of my products will convert best, and my product range may still be quite limited. If my site is great, my "real" qualified traffic is steadily increasing , and I still can't make a single sale, there's a few things I'd do before giving up. Firstly, I'd try to order a product myself to see if there were any technical problems during checkout. I'd also make sure that any bonus policies that I have in place (free shipping, warranty etc.) are clearly visible to all visitors to the site.

What are my prices like? Are they too high (I might try a sale for a few weeks to test lower prices)? Or are they too low (people don't tend to trust items they think are too cheap)? I might adjust pricing to see if that helps conversion.

(At this point I would also like to say that we've never had a site with regular qualified traffic that hasn't converted. So I can only comment on our actual experiences from this point on.)

Once products start selling, I'd keep a really close on everything that happens throughout the ordering, packing and shipping process. Different products are going to have different packaging and shipping requirements, and you often only find these things out at this point. They're never insurmountable, but you might have try different couriers and shipping companies, as well as different packaging materials to figure out what is going to work best and what will be most cost effective. I'd make the item trackable if possible, and make sure to update the customer when the order has shipped, with the tracking number. I'd also keep tracking the item to see how long it took to get to the customers.

I'd then contact the customer and ask them about their experience. Not like a "desperate" first time seller, but as though it's something you do with every single customer (which you may want to do anyway). Find out if they received what they expected (this will help you improve your photography and descriptions) and assure them that you'll fix any problems they might have had. Go above and beyond here, and don't hesitate to give them a refund if necessary, they shouldn't have to pay for your learning process.

From here on in, it's just a matter of testing and measuring. Test different prices, policies, product ranges and promotions. I'd find out which were my best sellers and make sure I have more of those in stock than my longtail products.

Constantly improving your branding is also important once you're starting to convert. Can you improve your packaging? Is there any additional items you can include with each order that will surprise the customer (in a good way!)? Can you improve your shipping and handling times or speed up your customer service? These factors seem small, but they are often the differentiating factors that allow you to charge a lot more than the competition, and still be more popular. Branding takes time and effort, but it is ultimately what will save you from getting into price wars with the competition, which usually results in both of you going out of business.

All throughout this I'm still commenting on blogs and in forums, and writing the occasional article. Even if I'm ranked number one in Google, I still want to get more traffic from longtail keywords that Google finds in my new content, and I want to make sure that when someone else finds my niche they reject it. Why? Because I'm the competition. And the competition is now too high.

Once I've sold a few products, traffic is still coming in, and it's clear I have a real business going, I'd want to start more. This time, I'd probably find a couple of new low competition niches and get them going at the same time. I now know it works, and I know what is involved to get them going. There is less risk because of this, and I want an empire, not just a single site. It's now become clear to me that while it may look like I have several online businesses, in my eyes I just have one, that happens to use several websites as the platform for selling different products.

So there you go, that's what we'd do, and that's still what we do. We often meet frustrated e-commerce site owners who believe they've tried all this, and it doesn't work. What we generally find out though is that they did everything mostly right... except that initial keyword research, without which you will find it extremely difficult to succeed.

"Takeaway Tips"

- Get started;

- Have patience;

- Keep building content;

- Reap the rewards.

Still have questions about the process? Feel free to ask us at
www.talknbusiness.com.

Chapter 11 - Applications We Use

Setting up your initial website or empire does not need to be costly. Here are the tools (mostly free!) that we use to run our empire. There are some significant omissions here (like hosting, domain name registrar, stock photo sites) because our preferred providers change over time. Please visit www.talknbusiness.com/tools-you-gotta-use for the most up to date software and service providers that we're using. Here are a few that are unlikely to change anytime soon.

Google Apps For Domains

This is like Gmail for businesses. It allows you to setup your email address(es) using your domain name (eg. bobsmith@mysite.com instead of bobsmith@gmail.com). This allows you to access your emails from anywhere with an internet connection. It also allows you to use Google Docs, which is a great way to store and share documents online, is very easy to use, and great managing outsourcing tasks. You can watch your contractors "live" as they update your documents.

The other great feature of using Google Apps For Your Domain is that each time you start a new business, you can add that domain as an "alias". This means that you can send and receive emails to and from all of your businesses from the one account. This makes it extremely easy to manage a lot of businesses (and social networking accounts) all from the one login.

Using Gmail also gives you access to all of the usual Gmail apps like to-do lists and calendar. Because it's so popular, you'll find it very easy to setup Gmail on mobile devices as well (particularly on Android based devices). It's a great tool, and we can't recommend it highly enough.

Open Office

Open Office is a free open source replacement for Microsoft Office, and it does an excellent job. We use it primarily for word processing, spreadsheets and presentations.

Skype

Another free service we can't live without. As we travel, Skype is not only a great way to keep in touch with friends and family, it's also a very cheap way of being able to phone customers from anywhere. While this service is not free, it is very cost effective.

Another way to use Skype is by getting an online number with them. This service (and you can get one in multiple countries), provides you with a local phone number that customers can call. To them it looks like any other local phone number, but it redirects the call to your Skype account. This means the customer only pays what a standard local call would cost, but you can receive the call anywhere in the world.

If you want to have a toll free number, you can redirect it to your Skype online number - and you can have toll free numbers all around the world - all of which funnel to your one Skype account.

Nvu

If you do feel like getting your hands dirty by messing with your website code (please backup first!), then Nvu is a good little HTML editor you can use. We're not coders ourselves, but using a tool like this can help you change some basic elements without having to get a contractor to do it for you. And of course, it's free!

GIMP

Strange name granted, but this a free replacement for Photoshop. Not quite as good or comprehensive, but if you still feel like doing some serious image editing, then GIMP is a great tool to help you do so.

Filezilla

Again, please be careful when messing with your website, but if you need to upload some images, or amend some files, you will need to access your hosting account using an FTP program. Filezilla is free, and is generally considered to be one of the best. We like it, and find that it's much faster than some others, and good for accessing multiple accounts at once.

Shortstack

Shortstack is a fantastic resource for customising your Facebook business page, as well as running social media competitions that fit within Facebook's strict rules.

As mentioned at the start of this chapter, some of the main tools we use aren't listed in this book, as we'd prefer to give you the most accurate information we can about the best tools to use. Head to:

http://www.talknbusiness.com/tools-you-gotta-use

Chapter 12 - Mindset

Your Life Will Change

Most of this book is really just us laying down our business model and sharing it with you. This is what people asked for, and is also what we would have wanted to see back when we first started muddling through. The problem is, what got us through was not just developing this model, but our absolute fierce desire to change our life. We could give this book out for free, and not one in a hundred people would even bother reading it, and of those that did, maybe one out of a hundred would actually apply it. We hope that you are that person! But we also had to overcome a lot of pressures to be where we are today, and have no doubt that you will face a lot of them as well.

As mentioned in the introduction, we were the perfect couple. Mid to late twenties, about to be on a combined income of over $200,000USD per year, and the respect of all of our peers as well as our parents and their friends. Reality? We would have spent 5 days of the week, 48 weeks of the year away from each other, living separate lives, for the rest of our lives, while living a life of "keeping up with the Joneses". But still, it would be a relatively risk free life right? Once we'd finished life on "easy", we could then restart the game and maybe try the "medium" difficulty level instead, to see if we could achieve something more. Oh, that's right, you only get one life!

Now, for the past five years we have lived between Thailand, Australia and New Zealand. We spend every day doing what we want, which includes the gym, the pool, and working on our businesses. And do you know what? We STILL get family and friends asking us when we are coming back to get a real job! We have been doing this for five years now, and we still have people trying to suck us back into the old life. They don't understand that we will never go back. Our life is 100 times more enjoyable, relaxing and rewarding than what it was, and you would have to drag us back kicking and screaming.

The point we are trying to make is that you need to understand that it is going to take some intestinal fortitude to embark on this journey, because you may not get the support you'd hoped for from among your friends and family. We've been fortunate enough to get great support from many of our close friends and family members, but there will always be those that don't understand what you are trying to achieve. Please don't let this stop you. Not now, and not one, two or three years from now. This is your life, and you only get one shot, so make it count.

You Will Fail

Okay, so that heading probably didn't fill you with confidence. In fact, if you grew up in the same type of school system that we did, the word fail is so strong that it would have instantly sparked a negative reaction from you.

Failing is a part of life, and is definitely a part of business. One of the main reasons we encourage you to build an empire instead of just one business, is because probably not all of them will be successful. All of the product and market research advice we can give will not spit out a business that is 100% guaranteed to succeed. It will make the odds of success much more likely, but you should go into this knowing that not everything you do will give you perfect results.

One great line that goes around business circles is "fail fast, fail cheap". That is pretty much our motto! It's why we give you the tools and the skills to scale into each business, so that if it fails, you lose as little capital as possible. We've seen people who seem to think that if they don't throw their life savings into the first business concept they find, the universe won't think they are committed enough, and will make the business fail. These people are usually chewed up and spat out pretty quickly, and we don't want you be one of those people. You don't have to "prove" yourself to the business. Instead, we want you to be a serial entrepreneur, and only spend increasingly more on a business when the business proves itself to you.

Just A Little Patience

Businesses take time to grow, so be prepared for it, both emotionally and financially. We give our businesses a year before we expect them to prove themselves to us. We now know that a website can sit dormant for months and months, with zero traffic, and then in one week jump to 50-100 unique visitors a day. Time to break out the champagne! Only drink half the bottle though, because you may need the rest of it to drown your sorrows when the opposite happens, and for some unknown reason your site falls out of Google love for a while. Ultimately this is why we recommend having a number of sites, because if one site goes down for a while, the others will provide that necessary balance that will help you sleep at night. The beauty of a well branded, well setup, "real" product site though is that Google slaps rarely happen anyway.

Perfection Is The Enemy Of Action

I read once that the Japanese tend to eat until they are 80% full, because they know that twenty minutes after eating, and the food finishes digesting, they will feel 100% full. We apply a similar concept when starting a business/marketing program/social media campaign/pretty much everything. If we feel we are 80% ready to go, then we launch. If we think the website is 80% to our liking, then we'll launch it and let the techs finish the job later. We do this on purpose, because we know that waiting for the final 20% to be finished will take as long as the initial 80% took. If you're waiting for the stars to align before you kick off, then you're going to be waiting for a long time. Only 80% sure about the supplier? Order anyway. Only 80% sure about the developer you've shortlisted? Hire them. You will have a few hiccups along the way by doing this, but you won't get anywhere at all if you don't.

Problems Are Opportunities

On that note, how you handle those hiccups that you come across (some small and some large) will be the difference between your success and failure. Business owners are problem solvers, bar none. The only reason any business can survive is because its owner is willing to solve problems that other people aren't. If you've hit a roadblock in your business, then look in the mirror and say, "I'm an entrepreneur, and this is what I do".

Chapter 13 - Bootstrapping In Style!

The term "bootstrapping" refers to starting a business on minimum funds. It means that you use as little of your own money as possible, and then try to grow organically (eg. using the funds generated from the business to grow the business, as opposed to putting more of your own funds in). There is no question that this makes for a much slower process, but this can be a good thing, as you will have to learn a lot yourself along the way, and rushing in can cause you to make a lot of mistakes. One of the advantages to this kind of business is that you can grow it on the side, while keeping your day job. The disadvantage is that keeping a day job means that you don't have the time, energy or "brain space" to devote to making your business a success.

Everybody's circumstances are different, particularly their family situations, so what we're about to suggest might seem a bit far fetched to many, but have you considered moving countries? In Australia for example, an online business earning $300 per week wouldn't even pay the rent, let alone let you quit your job. Here in Bangkok (where we are living at the moment), $300 can be a very comfortable weekly budget for two people, and you would be by no means giving up any luxuries. We live in a gorgeous little modern apartment in a gated complex. We have better, faster, cheaper internet than we had in Australia. We have our lunch and dinners cooked for us, we have a full gym on site, as well as three lagoon pools and a few putting greens. A third of our weekly budget is for massages, movies (in better cinemas than in Australia), shopping and dates, but best of all, we spend all day together working on the businesses that we love – full time. Sound like it's too good to be true? That's what we thought, and we waited far too long to make the move. A few weeks ago (at the time of writing) we spent a few days visiting Angkor Wat in Cambodia, which was a lovely little detour, and we are off to Hong Kong and China soon to visit our suppliers again (which is much cheaper and easier to do when you are already in Asia).

If somewhere like Bangkok doesn't appeal to you, there are numerous other places both in Thailand and other countries that are cheaper still, and it's a great way to get away from the peer pressures and other distractions of living in a western country.

The reality is, we now struggle with the idea of ever returning to Australia, as we would rather live a life between New Zealand and Thailand. We've also learnt that $1000 per week may not get you much in your own country, but with it you can live like a king elsewhere. What's even better is that with Skype, we see more of our friends and family now than when we lived near them!

Even if you don't want to make a permanent move, the ability to be able to build your businesses with no other distractions should be enough to make you at least consider the move. It also allows you to control your distractions (friends and family) and allows you the clarity of thought to carve out your own destiny.

A Final Word

What you have just read is the book we wish we'd had many years ago, as it would have saved us a lot of heartache, time and money, and we hope it will do the same for you.

What we haven't spoken about is the "why" of building your empire, and this is the most important question of all, as it will keep you going, even when things aren't going as well or as quickly as you'd hoped. Everyone has different reasons for embarking on a journey like the one you are about to begin, but most people don't seem to be after great riches, they just want more time. Time to spend with friends and family, time to pursue their hobbies and interests, and time to relax and enjoy life. It's our firm belief that the phrase "time is money" is a misnomer. Money comes and money goes, but time just goes. A friend once said to me that if you spend money, you can always make more, but the only thing you can do with time is spend it.

So spend it wisely.

Best Wishes

Nathan & Tessa Hartnett

Thanks for reading. If you have found the book useful, we'd love it if you were able to post a review of our book on Amazon. But before you do, if you have any questions that haven't been answered in this book, please contact us at www.talknbusiness.com, as we'd love to help, and update the book so that others can read the answers to your question(s) as well. If there is something that you are still confused about, chances are someone else is also asking the same question.

For continued updates to the information in this book, please visit www.talknbusiness.com.

For the most update information concerning the software and tools that we use, please visit www.talknbusiness.com/tools-you-gotta-use/

For more in-depth information on product sourcing, please read "The Retail Rebellion Product Sourcing Guide" also available on Amazon.com

Good luck, and let us know how your business is going!

Made in the USA
San Bernardino, CA
16 August 2013